Cricut Craft

Cricut Craft

25 beautiful makes for your home

Paula Milner

Contents

Noah
Florence

RUPERT'S SWEETIES
JENNY'S JAM
HANDMADE WITH LOVE
CHILLI POWDER
PINE NUTS
DRIED APRICOTS
ALMONDS
PUMPKIN SEEDS

Introduction

When I was first approached to start working with Cricut, I thought it was pronounced 'Cry-Cut'. I quickly realized that it is, in fact, phonetically pronounced: 'Cric-ket' (yes, like the sport or the bug!). It took me a long time to say it right....

I first heard this 'word' at a large craft festival at the National Exhibition Centre in Birmingham, UK, in August 2017. I was approached by a rather lovely lady called Kathy. She recognized me, and my then nine-month-old baby Freddie, who was strapped to me in a carrier. She asked if I was 'The Crafty Lass', and proceeded to explain that she had followed me for a while on Instagram. She worked for Cricut in the Marketing Team, and wondered if I would like to know more about it.

Before I knew it, I was very kindly sent one of the original Cricut Maker™ machines, an EasyPress™ and some materials to try out. I discovered this incredible machine could make almost anything! My crafting mind was blown. I went on to get making. I made many, many things: arty decorations for my children, personalized clothing, unique gifts for my friends and home décor for our family. I even made personalized shoes for the whole family and a very colourful umbrella!

In 2021 I went on to become one of the UK Cricut Crew members and began teaching workshops online and later face-to-face in shops. Most recently, I have become a Cricut Contributing Artist, designing digital files for the Cricut Design Space.

While Cricut crafting can, of course, be *incredibly* exciting, I also understand it can overwhelm. Once you first open that box, you see your beautiful new crafty toy, you want to dive headfirst into 'digital crafting'. But how? There is so much inspiration, so many ideas, lots of tools and accessories, and lots to learn.

So, where do you begin? I wrote this book for this very reason. *Cricut Craft* offers 25 beautiful projects to make for your home and as gifts. I have designed these projects with the aim of giving you a gentle start. Or, maybe you aren't new to Cricut but you need a refresh and some inspiration for you to get creating again.

I also offer further creative suggestions at the end of each project in 'Going Beyond The Make'. Whatever the stage of your Cricut journey, I want to be able to provide you with the confidence that you can truly make anything you set your mind to. Throughout this book, you will see that I use various machines, and types of tools and accessories, but these projects have also been deliberately designed so that they can be used by and/or adapted to suit as wide a range of cutting machines as possible.

It is important to note that Cricut is an innovator. What I write down here, in theory, could change by tomorrow! There can be sudden technological advances or software releases. Cricut is constantly pushing crafting boundaries. And while I say things 'change', everything only really gets 'added' to – extra ideas, extra innovation and improvement.

Cricut is also, of course, a company, a business – it wants you to invest in its machines, and buy its products. But it is much, much more than that. Cricut truly wants to inspire us, to connect with us. To create a whole Cricut community that pushes those crafting boundaries together!

Let's go for it! Let's get Cricut crafting.

Tools & Materials

CRICUT MACHINES

Although each machine has its own capabilities, with a few adaptations a lot of the functions can be used on all of the machines. For example, you might need to consider the overall size of the project, the relevant machine-compatible material and the specific machine cutting mat (if a mat is required for your chosen material). I currently use Cricut Maker™, Cricut Explore™, Cricut Joy™, Cricut Joy Xtra™ and several Cricut EasyPress™ machines, so I have experienced a wide range of cutting and heating capabilities. I use every single one of the machines for different projects and different reasons. Although I suggest the machine I've used for each project, you can of course adapt to your own, depending on its cutting capabilities. You may just need to adjust the size and type of the materials you use. If you are unsure which materials to use for your machine, head to Design Space™ for guidance, or Cricut.com for further advice.

CRICUT MAKER™ FAMILY

I have always thought of Cricut Maker as the 'all-singing, all-dancing, can-cut-anything machine', and it pretty much can. It can cut more than 300 materials! There are various tools it can combine with to cut, deboss, draw, score or engrave. It can cut fabric, felt, leather, wood and engrave metal. You imagine it, and I bet it can create it. Cricut Maker does feel like a monetary investment – they are not the cheapest of crafty machines. However, when you consider its capabilities and the crafting possibilities, it feels absolutely worth every penny. If you are an all-round multi-crafter who just knows you will use this machine regularly, across multiple material bases, it feels an absolute no-brainer to be your machine of choice.

CRICUT EXPLORE™ FAMILY

This is another powerful machine that can cut more than 100 types of material. If you know you are just not going to be able to fully benefit from or utilize Cricut Maker for its full cutting capabilities – and you would also like to make a more economically conscious decision – Cricut Explore is a great choice without a huge amount of compromise. It can still create a huge amount super-fast.

CRICUT JOY™ FAMILY

When Cricut Joy was first released, I questioned why I would need another machine, when I already have the 'make everything' Cricut Maker and Cricut Explore? Well, I was wrong. Arguably, the Cricut Joy family have become my hands-down favourite. They feel really accessible and easily portable, so they can sit beautifully on my desk at all times, ready for creating. They are good economic value and great for quick projects, such as card making, or smaller vinyl or iron-on makes. These machines tend to be my 'go to' machines unless I need to go for something specialist or more complex, or want to create much larger designs.

CRICUT VENTURE™ FAMILY

Wow, what a huge machine! This is the widest machine, with creating possibilities up to 25in (64.5cm) wide and up to over 72ft (22m) long. This would be an ideal machine for a small business that wants to create projects in a large format and/or in bulk.

Cricut Maker 3™

Cricut Explore 3™

Cricut Maker™

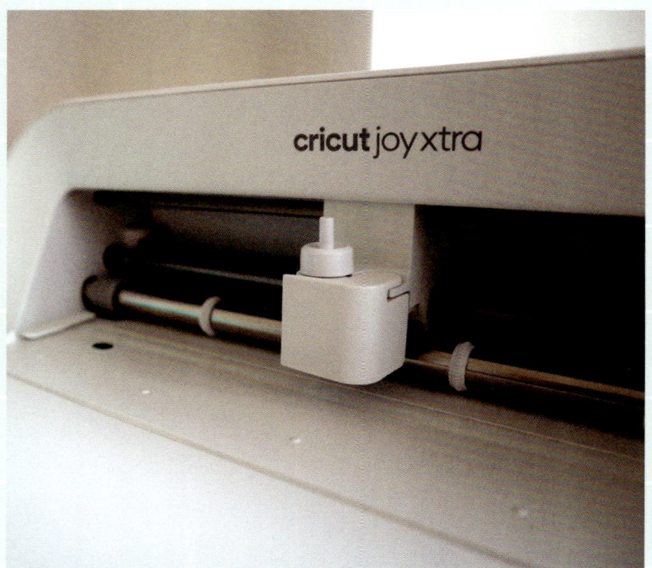

BLADES

Every machine comes with its relevant fine point cutting blade (above). Beyond this, there are various other blades, such as the rotary blade (above right) that can be incorporated for extra crafting possibilities – foiling, cutting fabric, debossing, perforating and so on. It all just depends on which machine you have, and what you want to create.

To change blades, you simply need to unclip the blade housing and pop your new one into position, before closing the clip again. Make sure to follow the on screen Design Space instructions (see page 12) as to what blade needs to be loaded for your chosen material (although, incredibly, Maker has sensors intelligent enough to understand what blade is in position to ensure you won't be able to load the wrong one!).

If you use a new type of blade in your machine for the first time, Design Space may ask you to do something called calibration. Just follow the on-screen instructions to allow your machine to set this up, ready for creating.

Some of the blades for Maker come with Quickswap housing. This is great as the main housing that clips into the machine is there and stays the same, but it allows you to quickly swap just the blade itself. And it can also save you money.

At some point, depending on how much you use each machine and blade, you will need to purchase replacement blades. If your cuts start being not 100% accurate – with gaps or not cutting at all – it is always worth trying a new blade first. Of course, if you still have problems, contact the Cricut Member Care team for further advice.

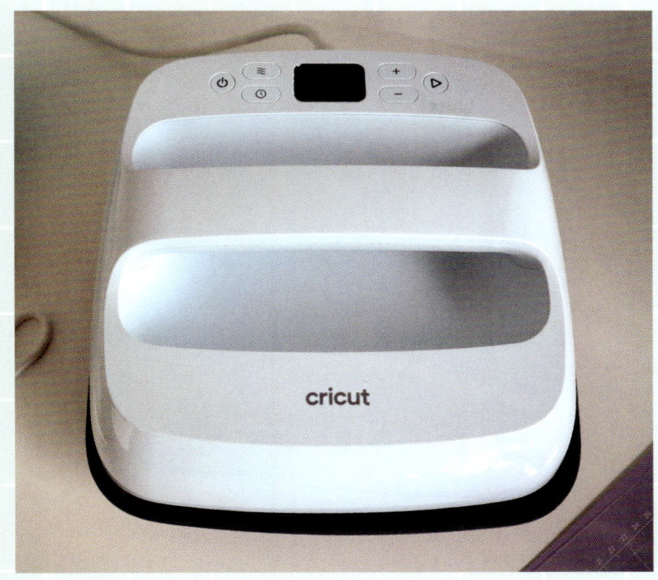

CRICUT EASYPRESS™

There are multiple models of this machine. From the tiny, compact Cricut EasyPress Mini™ to the much larger hot plates, such as Cricut EasyPress™ 3 (above) and Cricut Autopress™. There are also more bespoke versions, like Cricut Mug Press™ or Cricut Hat Press™, for example. Despite the radical size differences and capabilities, they all offer the same experience of extremely hot temperatures, across a smooth surface, that can be quickly adapted to the project and combination of materials you are using. You will need to use the official Cricut Heat Guide via the Cricut.com website for the most accurate and up-to-date advice when making a project that involves a Cricut heat press. There is also the Cricut Heat App, which can connect directly to some of the EasyPress machines via Bluetooth to communicate what settings are required. Then you really can guarantee you are heating your project correctly!

While it might seem frustrating that I have not provided all of the different heat guide information here in the book, and throughout the projects, it is important to have the best, and most relevant details for your own heat press version, the project you are making and the materials you have chosen. Advice can change, machines can update, so Cricut will be able to give you the most accurate and relevant information. They cannot advise on every parameter - even the room temperature and humidity could in theory affect your make - but the Cricut Heat Guide really is the go-to guide.

Please always make sure to keep your EasyPress on the recommended storage plate when switched on, as it can get extremely hot. And always create your EasyPress projects on a flat surface.

The main question I am asked about the EasyPress is: 'why can't I just use an iron?' And the straightforward answer is basically... an iron just isn't as good! A standard iron works, to an extent. I used an iron for my early iron-on projects, and quickly learnt how easily those projects peeled off, tore or simply didn't even adhere in the first place. On an iron, you cannot set the exact temperatures, nor do you have a precise timer that calculates the heat guide recommendations for your own unique combination of materials. An iron also usually has water/steam holes that will always affect the application of heat.

An EasyPress, whatever size and shape, has a super smooth heat plate surface that makes instant and direct contact with your project.

You may think that I work with Cricut, so of course I would be recommending the extra 'special' heat machines. While yes, I do work with Cricut, absolutely none of this book is 'recommended' under influence. This book is based on my own experiences and I would, genuinely, always use an EasyPress.

DESIGN SPACE

Once you open your new cutting machine and are ready to start getting creative, you will need to first install the Design Space app. You can use this on your phone, your laptop or your tablet. It is compatible with both Windows® and Apple Mac®. The layout and features slightly differ depending on which version you are using, but essentially they are all approximately the same. Design Space allows you to connect with your machine to create whatever you imagine.

You will need to set-up your new machine, connecting via Bluetooth or a cable depending on the age and type of device. It may ask you to complete various tasks for calibration and set-up, but it will show you what you need to do – just follow the on-screen instructions to get going.

From the Design Space homepage you can access ready-to-make projects, new images, fonts, ideas and crafty inspiration. You can find other Cricut crafters by searching for their profiles and follow them to see their ideas and journey (you can find me as The Crafty Lass!). You can also access help and further information here from the Cricut Member Care team.

Some of the pre-loaded and formatted projects allow you to click 'Make' and this will take you straight to the on-screen, step-by-step instructions for loading your materials and cutting straight away. However, you can also sometimes customize these by adjusting the sizes, colours and materials. If you choose to 'Customize', it will load the project onto the Design Space 'Canvas' where you can make any adaptions you want.

From the Canvas you can add images from the Design Space image library. There are thousands (and thousands!) of designs from Cricut and the Cricut Contributing Artist Team and that number is always growing. You can simply search using key words for what you need, and it will bring up anything deemed appropriate for your project. Or if you know the image's unique #M reference number you can search for this too. Just click 'Add to Canvas' for anything you want to use. You can also upload your own images to Design Space (as you will with the projects and exclusive imagery contained within this book). Click 'Upload' in Design Space following the on-screen instructions.

From the Canvas you can also add pre-designed templates, basic shapes, monograms, phrases or add your own text in a whole myriad of fonts. You can adjust sizes, change colours, and change the 'operation' type, such as changing from cut to draw.

One thing to note is, depending on your preference, you can change the units of measurement on the Canvas from metric to imperial (centimetres to inches) in the settings. For me, it depends on what I am making as to which one I use. I sometimes flip between the two. However, I find the grid lines on both the Canvas and the mats much clearer in inches. It will be totally up to you which one you prefer.

Once you have created a project on your Canvas you can save everything into Design Space too, under 'My Stuff'. This is great if you think you will want to make something again, or you want to make a project in stages and come back to it at any point. You can also share your makes within Design Space to give further inspiration to your fellow Cricut community.

Anything on the Canvas can be sent to your machine to create... so once you are ready to go click 'MAKE' and you are away!

Once your machine is connected, it will ask you a series of questions such as what material it is and the size of your mat etc. This helps the machine understand what blade needs to be installed, what pressure to cut at and whether it needs more than one 'pass'. Thicker materials need to be cut several times in the same position for the cut to fully pass through (as with the basswood cloud in the picture above right). Simply follow the step-by-step, on-screen instructions for loading your relevant mats and materials.

If there are any steps or processes you are unclear on, head over to the Cricut website and its Help Centre. There is a lot of up-to-date, useful information to guide you through anything you may need.

Design Space often requires updates. The Cricut team are continually making adjustments and changes to improve, add functionality and make things a more user-friendly experience. These updates will either kick in automatically when you shut down your application and restart again, or Design Space may give you a notification that it requires an update. Follow the instructions to install the update – just to make sure you have the latest crafty innovations and possibilities!

CRICUT ACCESS™

You may see something called Cricut Access being referred to or offered within Design Space. Cricut Access is a monthly subscription that grants you access to more image and font types inclusive of the subscription cost, as many times as you like. A lot of the images and fonts in Design Space are free to use anyway, so unless you plan on regularly creating a huge number of projects with a wide variety of imagery and text - such as for a small business, perhaps - you may require this subscription. If you want to use a specific font or image and you do not have a subscription you can purchase what you want to use for a one-off fee. The cost of each image or font will be listed on the relevant items, but you can keep and use it forever.

To begin with, I would personally recommend just using the free imagery and fonts to see how you get on. There is often a free trial for Cricut Access though, so you could always take up this offer. Then make, make, make as many things as you can in your trial period to see if you feel it would be useful. You need to consider what would work best for you and your own crafting needs.

IMAGES

Obviously to cut out shapes and designs - you need 'images'. These can come from a variety of sources, the projects in *Cricut Craft* use several different types.

Images need to be in specific file formats to be compatible with Cricut. If you head to Design Space, it will tell you what can be uploaded, or you can use available images from the Design Space library. These will have already been checked by the Cricut team, so are approved and ready to go.

DESIGN SPACE

Where I have used an image from the Design Space library, it will be my own The Crafty Lass design, as a part of the Cricut Contributing Artist Programme (CAP). I will have drawn these designs on paper, before translating them digitally and converting them to an SVG (Scalable Vector Graphics) file type - just ready for Cricut creating.

I have provided you with the image's relevant identifying name and number - such as 'Boats SVG #M490637EA' in the Tea Towel project on page 64. You can search for this image number in the Design Space library to add to your Canvas, or you can also access my Design Space images via my 'The Crafty Lass' profile page. As these images are part of the CAP, if you have a Cricut Access subscription, they will be completely free of charge. If you do not have the Cricut Access subscription they will be available for a small fee, as mentioned above. However, you are under absolutely zero obligation to use my images. You can use the relevant techniques in the project with whatever image(s) you would like: other free library images, or perhaps your own. I just hope the project designs inspire you to get creative.

BASIC SHAPES

In several of the projects, I have deliberately chosen to use the basic free shapes available directly on the Canvas. These shapes, such as the humble triangle, show how effective design can be created from such simple shapes. You can find the triangle in the Bunting project on page 148, or the hexagon, for example, in the Patchwork Cushion project on page 164.

EXCLUSIVE IMAGES

I have also included exclusive The Crafty Lass designs for you to upload yourself and get creative with. I have hand-drawn and digitally designed each one – as SVG files – especially for this book. These can be uploaded straight onto your Design Space Canvas to create the relevant projects. Of course, you could also adjust them, or use these images in other project ideas. I would be delighted to see how else you might get creative with them. I have suggested some ideas to get you started in Going Beyond The Make under each project. You can download the exclusive SVG files directly from the GMC website here:

https://www.gmcbooks.com/cricut-craft-downloads/

MEASUREMENTS AND COLOURS

The beauty of using SVG files in Design Space is that you can make them as big or as small as you like, duplicate them, change their colours or even their Cricut 'function'. So, you will note that I have sometimes listed the colours that I have used as a suggestion and/or I let you know approximately how many of each design or shape I have cut. But sometimes, I have deliberately not advised any exact measurements, as what you are planning to use the designs for will of course affect the quantity and sizes you cut. Make bigger, make smaller, cut many! You can do whatever you like with your images.

Citrus Table Setting, page 70

Rainbow Felt Banner, page 158

Botanical Towel, page 98

Toothbrush Holder, page 42

Autumn Garland, page 94

Homemade Jam Jars. page 36

Anemone Cosmetics Bag, page 114

Space Mug, page 58

Faux Leather Keyring, page 82

Children's Tableware Set, page 54

Wooden Weather Magnets, page 136

TOOLS & ACCESSORIES

MATS

A lot of materials need to be cut out on a Cricut cutting mat. If they don't need to be on a mat, they will be labelled as 'Smart'. You can see more on this later under Materials on pages 20-27.

Mats are available in a variety of sizes suitable to your machine and in various 'grips'. These are: StrongGrip (Purple), StandardGrip (Green), LightGrip (Blue), FabricGrip (Pink). There are also various card mats, which are very useful for specifically making greetings cards.

Each mat has slightly different 'stickiness' and you need to use the right one for your choice of material. For example, if you are using wood you will need to use a StrongGrip mat (bottom right) to really make sure your wood does not move around while cutting. With some finer paper materials you will need to use the LightGrip. This ensures your material won't tear when trying to peel and weed once your design is cut. If you are unsure what mat to use for your choice of material refer to Design Space or the Cricut Help section where there should be lots of advice on this.

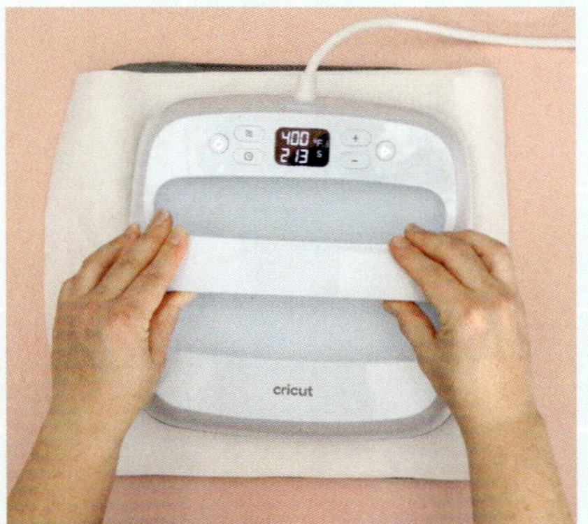

The mats are really bendy! Sometimes, it is best to bend your mat (instead of your material) so that your project comes away from the surface. This can help to ensure your project stays flat and does not tear.

If you ever need to measure anything to check how much material you might need on the screen compared with your mat, it is really handy to have the gridlines on the mat and the ruler on the side to check.

Each mat will come with a thin cover sheet. Make sure to always replace this once you have finished making. This protects the sticky surface from picking up excess dirt and dust.

You can use your mat over and over again, but it will start to pick up small fibres from your materials. Eventually, the mat will start to lose its sticky surface. However, did you know you can clean them? Just gently wash in hot, soapy water and leave to dry somewhere away from dirt and debris for them to regain their stickiness.

EASYPRESS MATS

There are specific heat mats for use with your EasyPress. These provide a soft, thick, flat surface for you to use when making your project with heat transfer. While you could achieve a similar result using something like a towel, an EasyPress mat ensures a consistently flat and firm area under your project. Always use a mat larger than your EasyPress plate size.

BASIC CRICUT TOOLS

1 Weeder: This is likely to be your most useful and used Cricut tool, which you use to remove any excess material from your cut design. It is very sharp and very precise.

2 Scissors: These are good-quality crafting scissors, which are handy for trimming materials when required.

3 Spatula: This is useful for lifting projects after cutting. The spatula helps ensure your project lifts away from a mat without tearing.

4 Scraper: This is a really useful tool for helping to clean excess weeded material from your mat. It is mainly used in vinyl projects to help transfer designs in combination with Transfer Tape.

5 Tweezers: Use these to lift up your materials or clean any rogue excess material from your mat.

6 Brayer: This is essentially a roller tool. I used to question 'why do I need this?'. Surely I could just firmly press my material into position using my hand? Well, I was wrong. The brayer really seems to be able to get things to adhere when it often doesn't seem possible. Your brayer can also gently push out any wrinkles or air bubbles trapped between your mat and material. I now always, always use my brayer!

7 Scoring Stylus: This is a really useful tool for doing exactly this: scoring! You can use in combination with your machine in the tool clamp or also manually with your hand as in the Paper Leaf Wreath project on page 88.

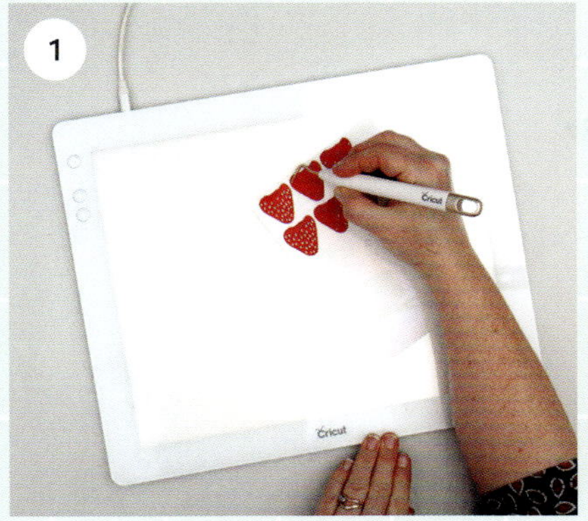

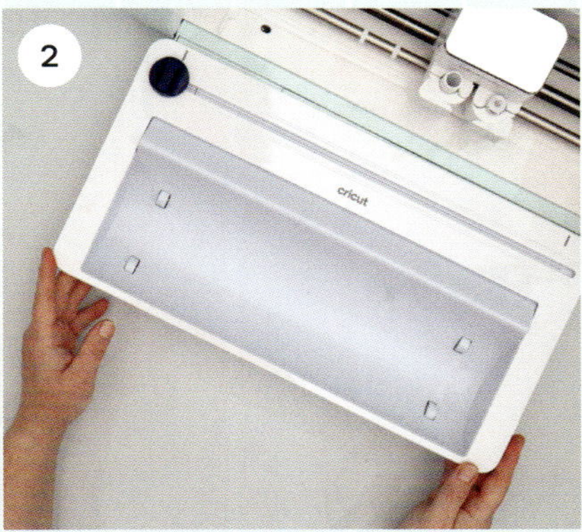

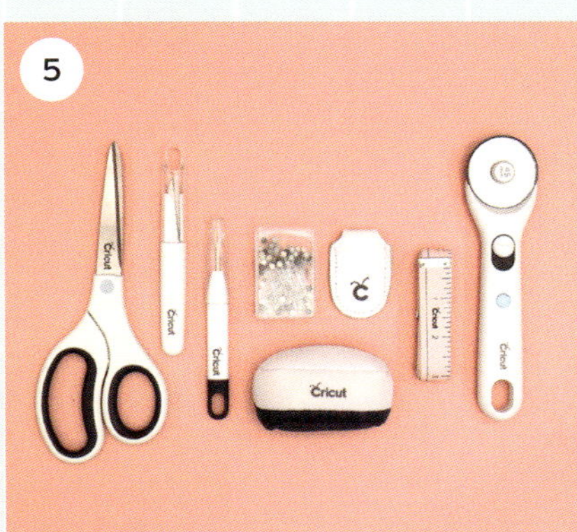

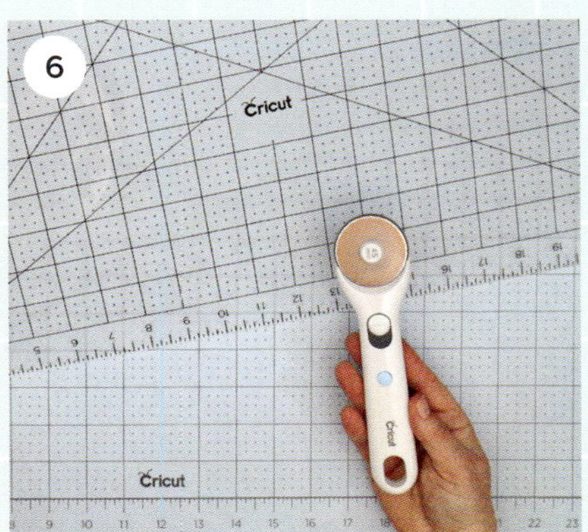

OTHER TOOLS

1 BrightPad™: Essentially a light box, this can be really useful when weeding more intricate designs.

2 Roll Holder: This is suitable for use with Explore™ 3, Explore™ 4, Maker™ 3 and Maker™ 4. It is super useful when using long rolls of Smart Materials (see the Personalized Doormat project on page 142). It comes with an in-built trimmer that is perfect for cutting straight lines when trimming back your material.

3 Foiling: Cricut foil transfer kits allow you to add delicate metallic touches across various materials. Make sure to purchase the relevant kit for your type of machine as there are different versions.

4 Pens: Your machines can draw too! Simply pop your pen into the relevant tool holder clamp and they will draw whatever you ask from Design Space, following the on-screen instructions. Make sure to purchase the pen sets that are relevant to your machine, as each one requires a slightly different size. There is also a washable pen, which is useful for fabric makes.

5 Sewing Kit: Cricut even have their own sewing kit. It comprises fabric scissors, thread snips, seam ripper, leather thimble, measuring tape, pins and a pin cushion and a rotary blade. I use this set throughout this book for any fabric and sewing projects.

6 Rotary Cutting Set: In addition to the machine rotary blade, Cricut also offer a hand-held rotary tool, alongside a self-healing cutting mat and an acrylic ruler.

MATERIALS & BLANKS

The amount of Cricut materials available is simply staggering. While I won't cover every single possibility, I will briefly cover some of the main materials and, at least, those used in this book.

SMART MATERIALS™

These materials have a super strong and thick carrier sheet. They can be directly loaded into your machine (right), without the need for a mat. They will specify what machine they are compatible with on the outer packaging as they will be size-specific.

Do keep any scraps of Smart Materials though. They can then be used by loading on to a cutting mat for smaller projects.

NON-SMART MATERIALS

If your material is not labelled as 'Smart', it will need to be cut on a relevant mat.

VINYL

Permanent Vinyl: Use this for items where you do not intend the design to be removed. It is weather, UV and water resistant. Once adhered to your project, make sure it doesn't come into contact with moisture for 24–48 hours to ensure the glue is fully adhered. Cricut would also advise to handwash any items, rather than using a dishwasher, if cleaning is required.

Removable Vinyl: Use Removable Vinyl for projects you may want to take off at a later stage. Peel away from your make, and if any sticky residue does reside, gently clean with a damp soft cloth to remove.

When cutting vinyl, whether Smart or on a mat, you will need to load the material with the shiny carrier sheet face-down, and the coloured vinyl face-upwards.

You can layer vinyl shapes/designs on top of each other, but I would recommend no more than three layers, otherwise it can become too thick.

If cutting simple shapes, you might be able to simply peel your vinyl cut outs away like a sticker (as in the Star Tumblers project on page 28). However, when creating a vinyl design where you wish to keep all the cut out elements in the same position, you will need to use Transfer Tape.

TRANSFER TAPE

This material, in combination with your scraper tool, helps you to move your cut-out shapes from the vinyl liner, and on to your blank or item. For the full step-by-step instructions for this you can see Transfer Tape used in several of the projects throughout the book.

There are two varieties of Transfer Tape.

Transfer Tape: the classic version, which is the best choice for the majority of your projects.

StrongGrip Transfer Tape: use this for textured vinyl, such as the Cricut Glitter Vinyl. I would highly recommend you don't use StrongGrip on other vinyl such as Everyday Vinyl: the glue is so strong, your project could tear or not transfer at all.

NOTE: When transferring your cut-out design from the carrier sheet on to the Transfer Tape, and when you are transferring your design on to your make blank, you should always try to pull the Transfer Tape at a diagonal angle. Move slowly to avoid tearing your design. If your design won't transfer, continue to use your scraper tool, to repeat the transfer process. It may just need a few goes! This is particularly true of Smart Materials, which I always find slightly trickier to transfer with their thicker carrier sheets.

IRON-ON

I think iron-on is my favourite Cricut material (if I really had to choose!). It is available in such a wide range of colours and textures, and I love how it offers the ability to create unique items very quickly. I have used iron-on for all sorts of personalized clothing for my boys and as gifts for friends. When using iron-on, you need a heat press to transfer your design.

When cutting iron-on, you will need to make sure you cut everything in 'Mirror' on Design Space. It should automatically default to this when you tell it what material you are cutting, but it is always worth checking. Everything will be cut in reverse before you place your design down on to your material – and it will then become the right way round once you have transferred. I have certainly been there – where I have cut everything the wrong way round and only noticed when I've gone to weed. You need to load your iron-on with the shiny carrier side face-down and the matte iron-on colour side face-up.

Beyond the standard Everyday Iron-On, there are various other types of iron-on to choose from: Glitter, Foil, Holographic, Reflective and even the specialist Sportsflex, which is suitable for use on activewear. There is also Express (which adheres quicker), Mesh and Mosaic, which has small patterns cut out. And patterned, with printed designs on. There is a huge array to choose from. Whatever you choose to get creative with, just always refer to the Cricut Heat Guide for the latest advice and information for your own materials combination.

Always wash your blank and make sure it is dust-free and thread-free before adhering your design. Washing removes any trace elements or chemicals in fabrics that may interact with how the iron-on transfers. I have learnt this the hard way! Always make sure that any iron-on is fully covered by a carrier sheet when heating as direct contact with an EasyPress plate could melt or burn the iron-on. If your iron-on won't adhere to the surface, simply repeat the heating process. Make sure you follow the instructions, from pre-heating your blank where necessary to the right timings and temperatures.

Layering Iron-On: Yes, you can layer iron-on. Cricut advise no more than four layers, but I would say three is enough. When layering, with each layer you add on the material adheres to itself. While two or three layers is perfectly fine, any more than this and it can create quite a stiff, plastic feel. It essentially loses its flexibility, which just doesn't look quite right. And if it is on an item of clothing, it can feel a little harsh or uncomfortable against your skin.

When layering up designs, you will always want to make sure any 'special' finish iron-on is the top layer. You shouldn't for example add Everyday Iron-On on top of Glitter Iron-On or Metallic Foil Iron-On. It will need to be the other way around.

Making sure all iron-on is fully covered by a carrier sheet when heating is particularly important in complex layered projects. However, also make sure to not 'trap' any small pieces of the carrier sheet under your iron-on in the heating process, as otherwise the iron-on may tear.

SPECIALIST VINYL AND IRON-ON

UV, Heat and Cold: Cricut also offer some super fun specialist UV, heat- and cold-activated materials, which change colour based on their temperature (above right). You can see the Heat-Activated, Colour-Changing Vinyl on page 58 with the Space Mug project. The planets change from purple to turquoise while you are drinking your cuppa!

Printable: Using your own printer, you can now also print on to some of the vinyl and iron-on varieties too! As long as you are using your own drawings, designs, photos or purchased imagery, you can print anything you like to get crafting with.

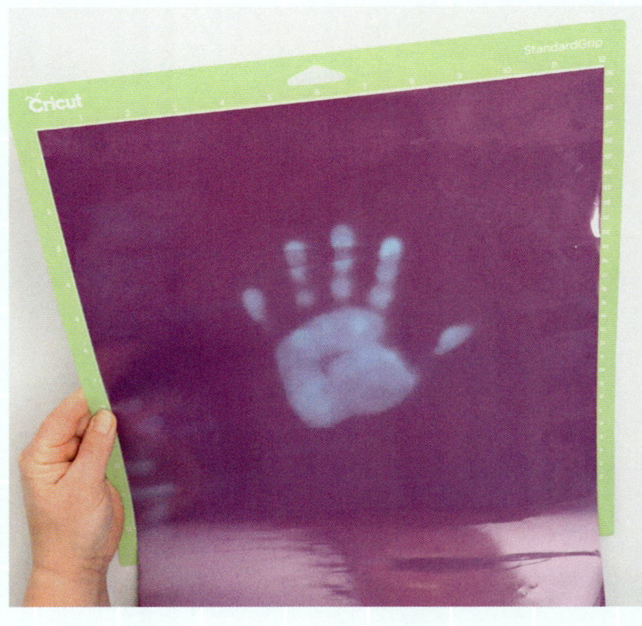

Stencil Vinyl: I have used Stencil Vinyl in the Personalized Doormat project on page 142. It cuts in a very similar way to standard vinyl, but I find it to be slightly thinner and it is also slightly clear, which helps when planning positioning. It is also much easier than vinyl to peel away and move if required.

INFUSIBLE INK™

This, I think is true Cricut 'magic'! Your colours and designs transfer physically inside the fibres of the fabric or ceramic surface.

Infusible Ink is available as Transfer Sheets or in special Infusible Ink pens that are compatible with your machines. Or you can use the pens to get drawing yourself.

The designs or drawings transfer under high temperatures and the results can be incredible. Vibrant colours are created that interact and embed into your blank to create permanent, washable and usable objects. I would highly recommend only using an

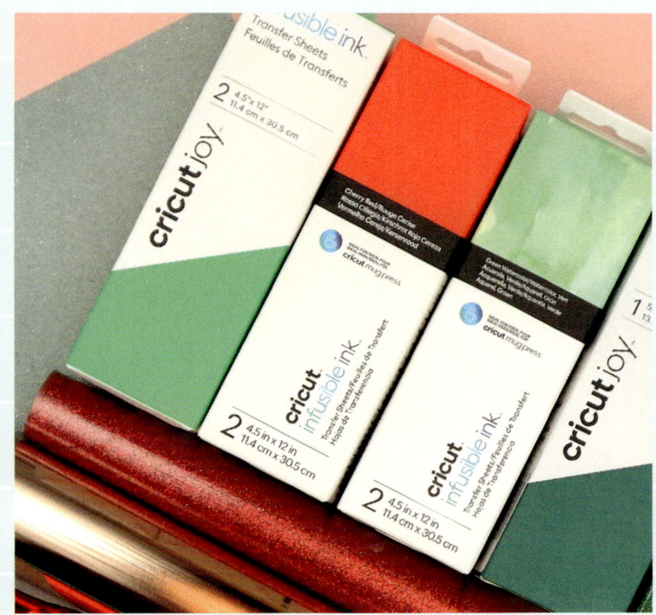

EasyPress alongside an EasyPress mat for Infusible Ink as Infusible Ink requires an incredibly high heat. A household iron simply would not have the consistent temperature level or smooth base plate to transfer your design smoothly. Cricut has some safety advice in place for using Infusible Ink. It advises that you should craft with it in a well-ventilated room, and also be extremely careful of the high temperatures you use to create your designs. For full details on this please read the information provided on each Infusible Ink product, or head to the Cricut website for the full guidelines.

Try not to move your EasyPress or project when heating Infusible Ink as it can cause your design to do something called 'ghosting', where your images appear one on top of the other in a shadow-type effect. Keep everything nice and still! Wait for a minimum of 24 hours before washing any Infusible Ink items to ensure your design is fully fixed into position.

INFUSIBLE INK TRANSFER SHEETS

Transfer sheets (above left) have a 'card'-type texture attached to a thin carrier sheet with the colours imprinted inside the paper. It is important to note that the colour on the Transfer Sheet will appear MUCH duller when you unroll it from the pack than the final results. So don't worry if it looks much paler.

Just like iron-on, you will need to ensure any designs are cut in 'Mirror' on Design Space. You need to load your Transfer Sheets shiny carrier-side down and matte coloured surface face-up on to your cutting mat.

INFUSIBLE INK PENS

Infusible Ink pens can be used to draw on standard printer or photocopy paper, which can then be transferred on to your blanks. Use your Cricut machine for the drawing stage, or get creative by drawing by hand. Note that whatever you draw will transfer in reverse, so be mindful of this, particularly if using any font.

BUTCHER PAPER

The Cricut Heat Guide will advise you to use something called Butcher Paper with your Infusible Ink projects (above left). It is a white, waxy paper that is often included with your Transfer Sheets inside the pack. Don't throw these pieces of paper away! If you have run out of Butcher Paper, you can also use standard brown parchment or baking paper, which has a very similar quality. It is really important to not skip using this as it helps protect your design under the heating process and it also helps to absorb any excess ink or moisture that can be emitted under heating. If the Cricut Heat Guide advises to use multiple layers of Butcher Paper, don't forget you can also fold it to layer up.

If you are creating a design that uses multiple layers of Infusible Ink, you may notice that some of the already transferred dye may transfer back to the paper. Just be super careful if you then lay any marked paper down on your project and reheat as it may re-transfer into your fabric where you do not want it to be. In an ideal world, you would use a new piece of paper for every Infusible Ink transfer, but in a project such as the Wreath Cushion on page 122 with multiple transfers this feels wasteful. Just be mindful of any dye within the paper, and perhaps even tear or cut any dye-stained paper away.

CRICUT INFUSIBLE INK BLANKS

Cricut offers specific fabric-based and ceramic blanks that are for Infusible Ink (above right). While you can, of course, experiment with other products, my own experience often shows that the designs may still transfer but the design may be duller or, in the worst case, patchy.

If you are looking for fabric, or fabric-based products, they will need to have a high percentage of polyester content, such as the Botanical Towels project on page 98. You could try on other ceramic blanks and it can work on some wood types too, but with mixed results.

HEAT-RESISTANT TAPE

When working with some of the EasyPress projects, such as the Ceramic Coasters project on page 102, Cricut offers something called Heat-Resistant

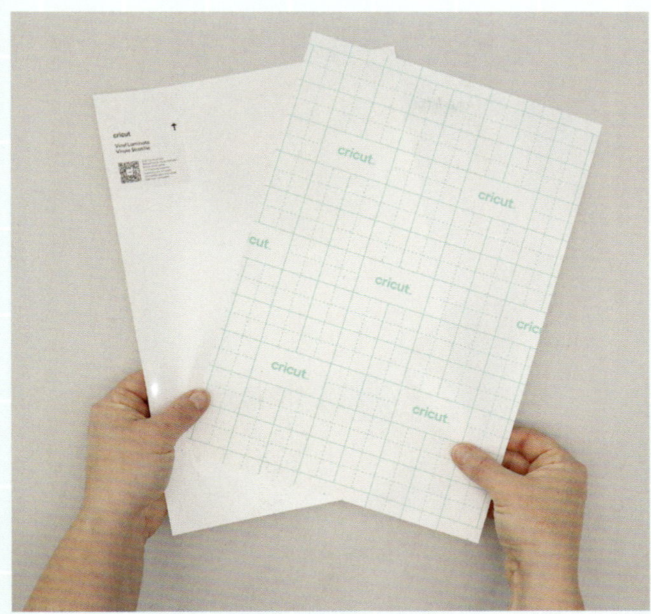

Tape. This is very thick and, yes, very resistant to the temperatures it can endure under an EasyPress plate. It really is useful for keeping things in position. Don't try to substitute this for masking tape or any other sticky tape under any circumstances. I have learnt this the hard way – they will melt and make a big mess!

LABELS

While you can get labelling everything you own using vinyl (such as the Storage Jars on page 48), Cricut also has some fantastic products specifically for labels in various finishes. These products allow you to write on them too and are almost instantly smudge free! You can see these in the Jam Jars project on page 36.

STICKERS

My boys absolutely LOVE stickers – I mean, who doesn't! You can make paper ones, waterproof, even holographic versions. Just like printable iron-on and vinyl, you will need to make these in the 'Print then Cut' function in Design Space using your own printer. I have created some Tractor and Daisy stickers in the Lunchbox and Water Bottle project on page 130.

PAPER

You can cut all sorts of papers and cards on your Cricut machine, just make sure to use a LightGrip mat or a StandardGrip mat that may have lost some of its stickiness. Cricut offers its own papers and cardstock but you can use any type of paper. You can see paper projects in the Autumn Garland on page 94 and the Paper Leaf Wreath on page 88.

FABRICS

Cricut Maker is your 'go to' fabric-cutting machine, in combination with the rotary blade. You can get creative with a huge array of fabrics, from silk, to denim, to foam. Cricut offers its own printed fabric packs, but you can use whatever fabric you like. In the projects in this book, I have chosen to use 100% cottons. You can find these in the Bunting project on page 148, the Patchwork Cushion on page 164 and the Reusable Face Wipes on page 154. Cricut Explore can also cut 'bonded' fabrics (non-woven) using the special Bonded Fabric Blade. If you do not have a fabric-cutting compatible machine, these projects could be adapted to be cut by hand using a cutting mat, ruler and hand-held rotary blade.

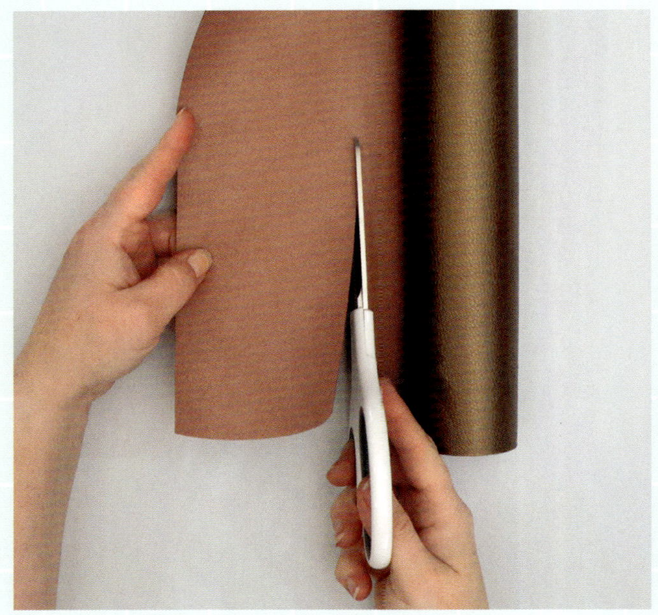

FELT

You can cut felt with Cricut Maker and Cricut Explore. In the Rainbow Banner project on page 158, I have chosen to use Cricut's own felt, which is a little stiffer than your classic soft woollen felt. It is sometimes advised to use the standard fine-point machine blade to cut felt, but I find the rotary blade a much better choice. The rotary blade slides over and through the surface of the felt rather than tearing through the material.

LEATHER AND FAUX LEATHER

While Cricut Maker and Cricut Explore can cut leathers using the deep-point blade, it surprises me how easily you can cut faux leather with any of the machines, including the Cricut Joy family. I used my little Cricut Joy and its standard blade for creating the Faux Leather Keyring project on page 82.

WOOD

I find it incredible that you can even cut some varieties of wood with Cricut Maker! You will need to make sure when selecting your material in Design Space to select the correct depth of your wooden sheets to ensure it calculates the amount of pressure and the number of passes it needs to do with the knife blade. When using wooden sheets, you need to use the StrongGrip Mat to make sure it does not move around. Also, use masking tape to further secure it in position.

On your machine you have little white star wheels on your machine track, which you can move. It is really important that you gently slide these to the right-hand side before you begin cutting thicker materials such as wood. Otherwise, your material may mark. You can simply slide the star wheels back again once you are finished. I use wood in the Weather Magnets project on page 136. If you don't own a machine compatible with the knife blade, instead of buying wooden sheets, you could buy some pre-cut small wooden craft shapes, and personalize them with a Cricut vinyl design or font.

OTHER TOOLS & MATERIALS

There are so many other materials, such as metal and acetate, and all sorts of exciting things that the machines can make with and do (even engrave, etch and deboss). I hope this has given you a broad overview of the materials used throughout these projects.

There are various other materials and tools that I have used, such as masking tape, paints and a hot glue gun. These are listed under each relevant project. There are three makes that use a sewing machine. These are the Bunting (pages 148–153), Resuable Face Wipes (pages 154–157), and the Patchwork Cushion (pages 164–173).

NON-CRICUT MATERIALS

While there are other materials and other blanks available in the digital crafting market, I can be truly honest and say that I have absolutely no idea whether these will work. I am sure some of them are great, and some, not so much. Personally, I have always stuck to the Cricut materials. I have worked with Cricut a long time now, and I KNOW the materials are right for the project. Why would I try anything else?

NEW TOOLS AND MATERIALS

Inevitably, Cricut will continue to add new and exciting additions to both their tools and compatible materials. For anything not mentioned here, or for further information, head across to the Cricut Help Guide.

STORAGE

STORING YOUR CRICUT VINYL AND IRON-ON

Try to keep your materials either flat, if smaller pieces, or rolled up in their original tubes if easier. You need to store them where you can limit any damage to the surface of your vinyl or iron-on. I keep mine in large-lidded storage containers, which keep them away from moisture. Try to store at room temperature.

STORING YOUR INFUSIBLE INK

Once your Infusible Ink packets have been opened and they are exposed to light they can be susceptible to damage. So it is really important to reseal any Transfer Sheets back in the dark packaging it originally came in. Store in a dark place, at room temperature, away from any moisture. If you keep scrap pieces or store your Infusible Ink for long periods of time, you should always test a small scrap piece before heating on a larger project to make sure it still works as expected. Sometimes there is a small square piece of fabric included within the packaging that allows you to do this. Otherwise, you will need a high polyester piece of fabric for testing. While I would expect opened Infusible Ink to deteriorate, I have stored open packets of Infusible Ink in their original packaging, in a dry space, for over 2 years and they still work correctly!

STORING YOUR MACHINES

Just like your materials, store your Cricut machines indoors at room temperature and away from moisture.

ISSUES

If you ever have a problem with your Cricut machine, contact the Cricut Member Care team for advice and support. There is a huge amount of advice on the website too. This ranges from step-by-step guides, answers to all the Frequently Asked Questions and, of course, all the latest machines, tools, materials and inspiration.

Star Tumblers

★ ★

This simple starry project, using coordinating glass and vinyl, really makes these beautiful tumblers sing! The glasses would look lovely dotted throughout your table décor. These ones are actually quite wide, so they could even be used for desserts, snacks or some lovely home storage. This is a great example of a 'scraps' project, where you can turn small pieces of vinyl into a beautiful product. I will be gladly keeping these in my kitchen, but I might make some more sets, as they would make beautiful presents.

YOU WILL NEED

MACHINE

- Cricut Machine and Blade (I used Cricut Joy and Fine Point Blade for Cricut Joy)

TOOLS

- Cricut StandardGrip Mat (if not using Smart Vinyl™)
- Cricut Weeder
- Cricut Scissors
- Cricut Spatula (optional)
- Cricut Tweezers (optional)

MATERIALS

- Cricut Permanent Vinyl in your choice of colours
- Glass Tumblers

IMAGES

- Design Space Basic Free Star Shape

NOTES

- If you are using Smart Vinyl, you don't need to use a mat.
- While this project is made with glasses, this could also be made using plastic or melamine cups.

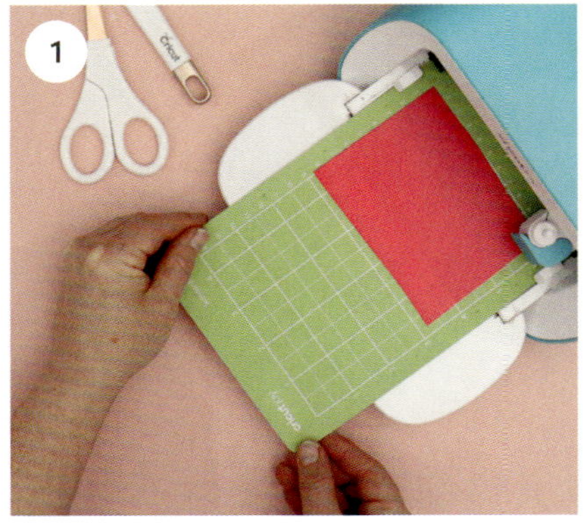
1

2

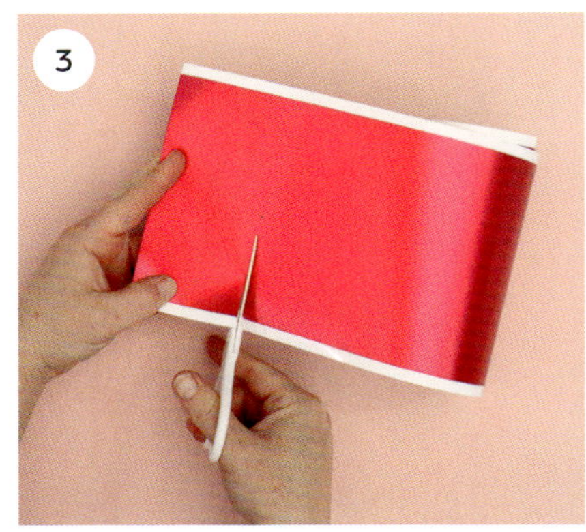
3

4

5

6

1 Open Design Space and create a star (available in basic shapes) on the Canvas. I have made each one around 1in (2.5cm) wide. For each glass I used 2 different colours of vinyl. One is slightly glittery and the other metallic. I have created 4 stars and followed the on-screen instructions to make the project twice for each glass, so there are 8 stars for each glass in total. Here, I have chosen to cut down some larger pieces of vinyl for use on the mat to best use the existing materials I have. Load your vinyl on to your mat.

2 If using Smart Materials follow the on-screen instructions to cut your stars without a mat.

3 Where required, trim your cut stars from the roll (or any larger sheets of vinyl).

4 I find, particularly with the Smart Materials, there is often a short band of unused vinyl before your design is cut out. Make sure to cut these off, and any other small vinyl pieces to save for another project.

NOTE I am actually collecting these small pieces to use in the Confetti Artwork project on page 32. Even small pieces of scrap unused vinyl are useful!

5 Weed any excess vinyl away from your stars using your weeder.

6 Decide which vinyl colours to use with which glass.

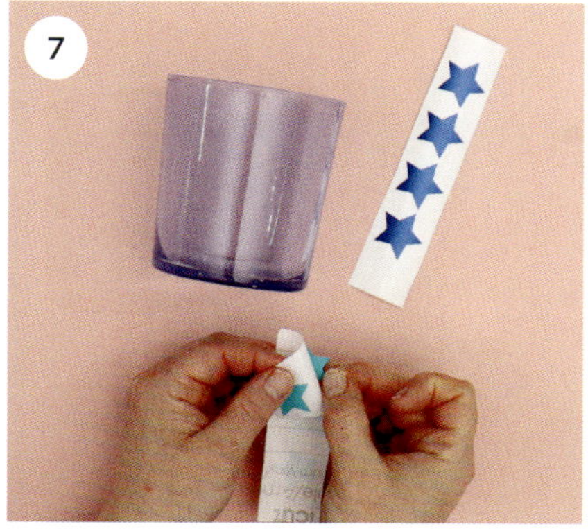

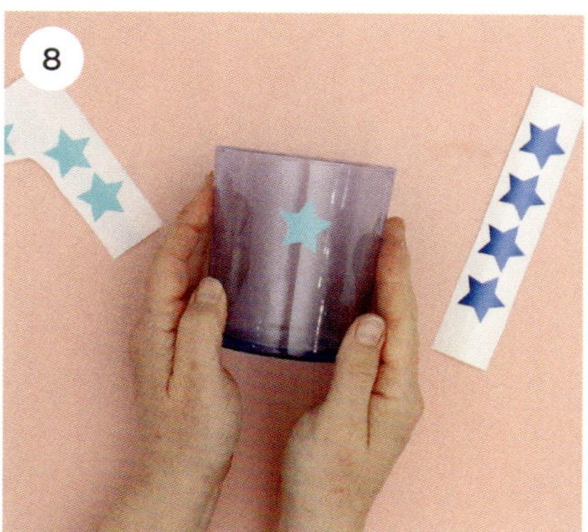

7 The great thing about using simple shapes like these stars in vinyl is that you don't need to use any Transfer Tape. You can simply peel each star away from the carrier sheet.

8 Make sure the outside of your glass is nice and clean and dust free. Place the star on your glass, wherever you like. I would recommend you don't place it too near to the top of the glass where you drink, but anywhere else would be fine!

9 Continue to add the stars around your tumbler.

10 Repeat with all of your other tumblers.

11 Sometimes it can be slightly more difficult to remove shapes from the Smart Material liners – you can use either your tweezers or spatula to help with this.

12 And you are done. A lovely set of starry tumblers!

NOTE Make sure you wait 24–48 hours before contact with water, such as washing or drinking from the tumblers. This allows the vinyl to be fully fixed. I would recommend hand washing these only.

GOING BEYOND THE MAKE

The basic star shape could be used in all sorts of ways: you could cut paper stars to make a garland, or perhaps you could cut stars out of iron-on or even Infusible Ink to make a cushion!

THROW
KINDNESS
AROUND
LIKE
CONFETTI

Confetti Artwork

I love this simple artwork, which uses a vibrant mix of vinyl. If you use removable vinyl, you could continue the confetti onto the surrounding wall. This frame is clear on both sides, and it looks lovely on a windowsill with sunshine shining through.

YOU WILL NEED

MACHINE

- Cricut Machine and Blade (I used Cricut Explore and the Fine Point Blade for Cricut Explore)

TOOLS

- Cricut StandardGrip Mat (if required)
- Cricut Weeder
- Cricut Scissors
- Cricut Spatula
- Cricut Tweezers (optional)
- Cricut Brayer (optional)
- Cricut Scraper (optional)

MATERIALS

- Cricut Vinyl in your choice of colours
- Cricut Transfer Tape
- Frame

IMAGES

- Design Space Basic Free Circle Shape

FONT

- ITC Busorama

NOTES

- I have collected lots of small scraps of vinyl, in a mix of permanent, removable, textured and holographic, and in both standard and Smart. I wanted to use lots of different colours, and as I am not planning on removing this vinyl, I don't think the mix matters!
- To create the bold effect with the type, I used the 'offset' function in Design Space, to offset the text by around ¼in (6mm). Of course, you can choose whatever font and effect you would like.
- Do remember that if you are using removable vinyl, ideally your project should not come into contact with water.

1 Add a circle shape to your Canvas in Design Space and duplicate as necessary. Choose your font and add the text: 'Throw Kindness Around Like Confetti'. Follow the on-screen instructions for cutting out the font. I chose to use black vinyl for this to stand out and contrast with all the other bright colours.

2 Next, add your cut-out scraps of vinyl to your mat if required, or load your Smart Vinyl as necessary. If using multiple types of vinyl next to each other like this, try to group them by type, so you can advise Design Space what type of material it is. It will then adjust the pressure accordingly and cut the circles out correctly. I cut around 30 circles of $\frac{3}{16}$in (5mm) and 30 circles of $\frac{9}{32}$in (7.5mm) across multiple scraps on the one mat. I repeated cutting out the circles like this several times, to make sure I had a wide variety of colours. However, I did end up with a few left over, so perhaps adapt to your size of mat.

3 Prepare your frame for attaching the vinyl. As my frame is clear on both sides, I removed the two panes of central glass and put one to one side. Make sure your glass is nice and clean and dust free.

4 Trim around your cut-out font design and reserve any spare vinyl for another project. Weed your font using your weeder. The weeding tool is particularly useful for removing the smaller and more fiddly parts inside letters.

5 Weed the excess vinyl from around your circles.

6 Attach a piece of Transfer Tape to your font design, using your scraper tool to help it adhere. You can do this both front and back if it helps to move your design from the liner on to the tape. It also helps to do this against a hard surface such as a smooth, flat table.

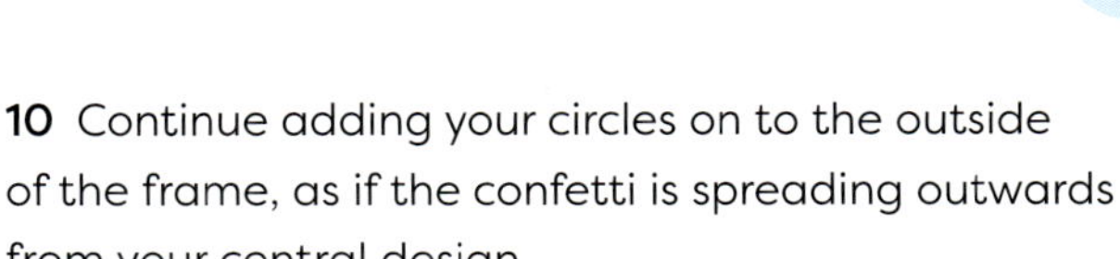

7 Peel back your design and the sticky Transfer Tape from the liner. Place centrally on to one of your glass panes (or your card if doing it this way) and firmly push into position before peeling back the tape.

8 Begin to stick your circles around your font, scattering the colours randomly. Continue to place the circles around your central text – you could overlap some if you like. I have tried to keep the placement quite random and not evenly spaced apart, as if it was real confetti being thrown. You can place as many or as few as you like on to your glass; I think it looks very effective with a nice mix of sizes and colours. Once you are happy, move on to the frame.

9 Place the other pane of glass on top, before placing everything back into the frame.

10 Continue adding your circles on to the outside of the frame, as if the confetti is spreading outwards from your central design.

11 And you are finished! A lovely piece of colourful confetti artwork.

GOING BEYOND THE MAKE

If you wanted to use a standard frame, you could create the artwork on card before framing. Be careful if using card that the Transfer Tape doesn't attach to it and tear your card. Try to make sure it is a saved and re-used piece of tape so it is not as sticky as when new. You could also try this project in iron-on. It would make a fabulous and fun T-shirt design!

RUPERT'S
SWEETIES
JENNY'S JAM
HANDMADE WITH LOVE

Homemade Jam Jars

This project would make a fabulous handmade, personalized gift. If jam making isn't your thing, there is also the option to switch up the project for these jars to hold sweeties too. You could adapt the text on each label to be unique to the recipient. These would also look lovely to use in your own kitchen!

YOU WILL NEED

MACHINE

- Cricut Machine and Blade (I used Cricut Joy and Fine Point Blade for Cricut Joy)

TOOLS

- Cricut StandardGrip Mat (if not using Smart Vinyl)
- Cricut Joy Pen
- Cricut Weeder
- Cricut Scissors
- Cricut Scraper
- Fabric Scissors or Pinking Shears (or a machine that can cut fabric)
- Cricut Tweezers (optional)
- Cricut Spatula (optional)
- Cricut BrightPad (optional)
- Cricut Cutting Mat and Hand-Held Rotary Blade (optional)
- Pencil (optional)

MATERIALS

- Cricut Joy Smart Label™ Writable Vinyl
- Cricut Permanent Red Vinyl
- Cricut Permanent Green Vinyl
- Cricut Transfer Tape
- Jam Jars
- Fabric
- Rubber Band
- Ribbon or Elastic (optional)
- Additional Decoration such as Strawberry Buttons (optional)

IMAGES

- Exclusive Strawberry SVG
- Design Space Label SVG (hearts) #M505D85CA or Label SVG (stars) #M505D85CB

FONT

- Close to My Heart - You Are Here

NOTES

- Make sure you use clean, fully sterilized jam jars so they are safe for storing food.
- If changing to the sweetie version of this make, simply swap out the exclusive Strawberry SVG for the Sweeties SVG and change to whatever colour vinyl and fabric you would like.
- You could swap your Permanent Vinyl for Removable Vinyl depending on whether you would like to have the option to later remove the jar decoration.
- This project uses my 'Label' image in Design Space. You could use this technique with whatever image or shape you would like.

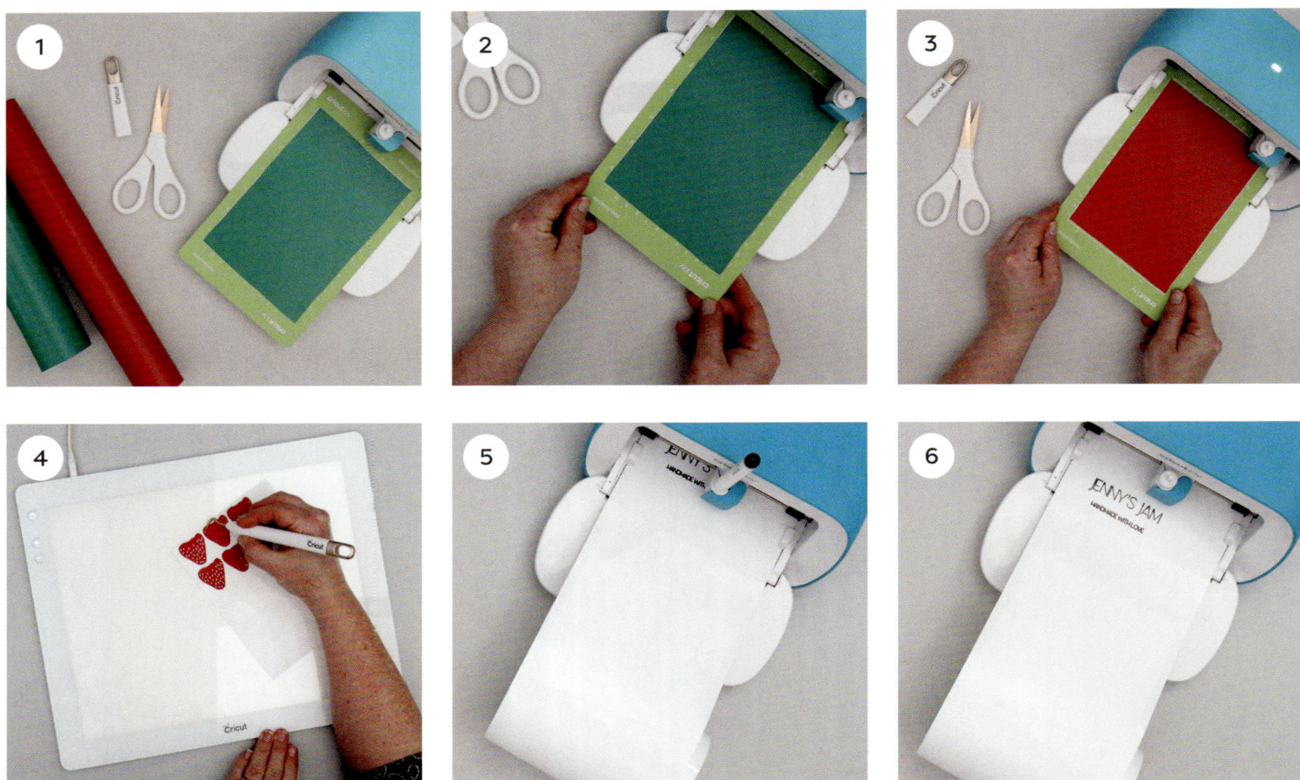

1 Upload or access the exclusive SVG files or Design Space images.

2 Duplicate the strawberry design as many times as you require in Design Space. I have used 6 per jar. Follow the on-screen instructions for loading your materials and cutting out your design.

3 Change colour when requested. Your Design Space may do this in a different colour order. This is absolutely fine, as long as all the relevant colours are cut.

4 Weed any excess vinyl away from your design. I am using the BrightPad here to help weed the fiddlier parts. I find it useful to highlight the cut lines.

REMINDER If using a mat, remember to put the liner back again to keep it clean.

5 Make the label using your Smart Label Writable Vinyl, machine-compatible pen and the Fine Point Blade and housing. As you are using a Smart Material this time, you don't need a mat. In Design Space, access the label images, or choose what label shape you would like. Choose the font you would like to use for your label. I have chosen this one as it is nice and clear, but you can use whichever font you prefer as long as it is 'Draw' function compatible. Type your personalized text and make sure you set the function to 'Draw' in Design Space. Align your text where you would like it to sit on your label and use the 'Attach' function in the Canvas to ensure everything lines up correctly. Follow the on-screen instructions to create your label.

6 Switch from drawing to cutting when requested by unclipping the machine clamp and replacing the pen with the blade. You will notice that the pen writing is dry already: no smudging!

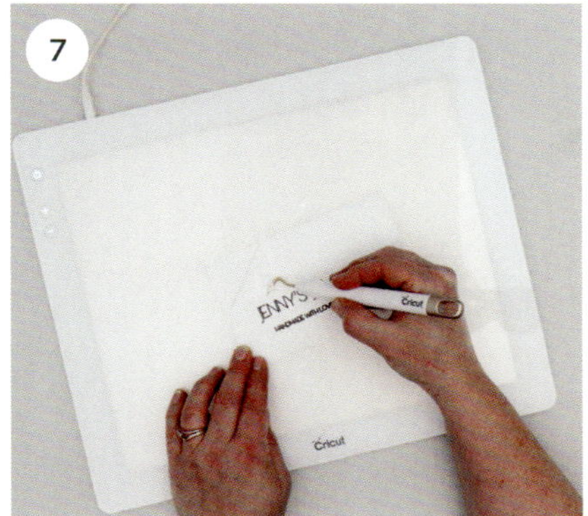

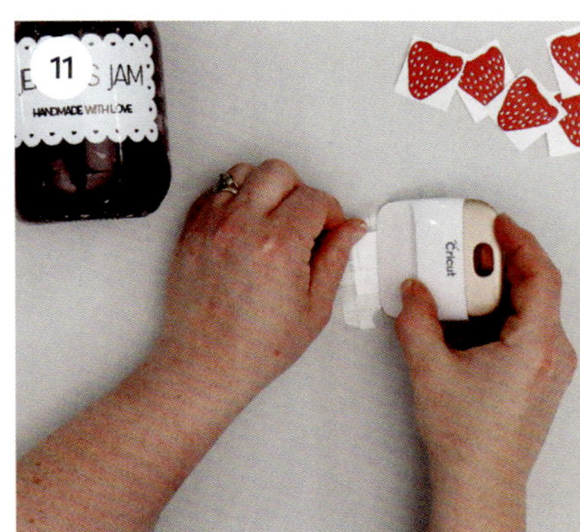

7 Trim the Smart Material from the roll, if you need to, and weed any excess vinyl away from your design using your weeder. Again, I am using the BrightPad here to weed the fiddlier parts.

8 Now you are ready to decorate your filled jar. Make sure the outside of your jar is clean and dust free. Gently peel your label away from the liner before placing on to your jar. I have used the top of the jar as a guide to help me line the label up straight. Try to go slowly when peeling Smart Label Writable Vinyl so it doesn't tear.

9 Cut out each strawberry and the tops ready to transfer on to your jar.

10 Now take a small piece of Transfer Tape: cut only a small square just bigger than your strawberry. You can reuse this one piece multiple times! Peel back the tape from the liner.

11 Add your tape onto one of the strawberries and using your scraper, push your design down on to your tape. You can do this both front and back if it helps to move your design from the liner on to the tape. It helps to do this against a hard surface such a smooth, flat table.

12 Peel away the white liner to reveal the design on your Transfer Tape.

13 Place your strawberry on to your jar wherever you would like and smooth down onto the glass. Gently peel away the Transfer Tape, leaving your strawberry design on the jar. Smooth out to ensure there are no air bubbles trapped underneath it.

14 Repeat with one of the strawberry tops using the same piece of Transfer Tape, aligning on to the strawberry.

15 Repeat with as many strawberries as you would like, I have just dotted them around the jar. I have used 6 in total. There are 5 going around the jar and 1 on the lid.

16 Instead of the strawberry on the lid, you could add a vinyl label with the date you made the jam.

17 Now select your fabric, cutting mat and either your fabric scissors or hand-held rotary blade. Alternatively, you may prefer to cut your fabric using a fabric-compatible Cricut machine.

18 You need to cut a circle of fabric large enough to go over and around the jar lid and slightly down the sides, which you will secure in position with a rubber band. I find the easiest way to do this is to begin by cutting a square. Using your jam jar as a guide, cut into the fabric allowing for some additional measurements around each edge. It doesn't need to be perfectly square, and the exact measurements will vary depending on your jar size. If you cut it slightly too big, you can always trim back the fabric later if needed. My chosen gingham fabric certainly helped to cut straight lines!

19 Once you have cut your square, you can cut each corner into a curve, creating your circle. If you prefer, you could use a pencil to draw these curves first, before cutting them out.

20 Place your fabric circle over your jam jar and secure into position using a rubber band. You could add some additional ribbon and decorations.

21 I have chosen to thread some cute little strawberry buttons I had onto some thin red elastic before tying the elastic into a bow.

22 And you are finished! A lovely, decorated jam jar.

GOING BEYOND THE MAKE

These strawberry and sweetie SVG files would look fabulous in iron-on.

You could use them in the Daisy Apron project on page 108.

You could also use this label shape for organizing items in your kitchen or files in your home office.

Toothbrush Holder

Brighten your bathroom with this simple vinyl project to create a tropical underwater world. Seeing all these bright colours every morning and evening would make me smile! Utilizing all sorts of permanent vinyl, this would again be a great 'scraps' project, enabling you to create something beautiful from all your saved leftover scraps.

YOU WILL NEED

MACHINE

- Cricut Machine and Blade (I used Cricut Joy Xtra and Fine Point Blade for Cricut Joy Xtra)

TOOLS

- Cricut Joy Xtra StandardGrip Mat (if required)
- Cricut Weeder
- Cricut Scissors
- Cricut Tweezers (optional)
- Cricut Brayer (optional)
- Cricut Scraper (optional)

MATERIALS

- Cricut Permanent Vinyl in your choice of colours
- Cricut Transfer Tape
- Glass or Plastic Tumbler

IMAGES

- Exclusive Fish SVG
- Exclusive Corals and Seaweed SVG
- Exclusive Starfish SVG

NOTES

- I have chosen to use a mix of vinyls. If you are using Smart Vinyl, you will not require the use of a Cricut mat.
- As this make is likely to be in contact with water, make sure you use Permanent Vinyl and not Removable Vinyl so that it can withstand this.
- I have used a large glass tumbler, but you could make this on a plastic cup instead if preferred.
- I chose this glass in particular, as it has a blue ombre effect that reminded me of the real sea. It also has little bubbles trapped beneath the glass, which felt very appropriate for these designs!

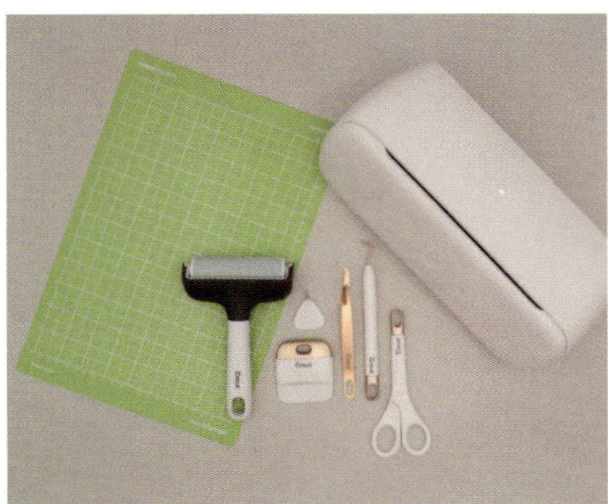

1 Upload the relevant exclusive SVG files to your Design Space Canvas. You will need a compatible mat (if not using Smart Materials) and your chosen vinyl colours. I have chosen to use a mix of Smart Materials and to also cut down some larger pieces of vinyl for use on the mat to best use the existing materials I have.

2 Trim your materials, if required, before following the on-screen instructions for cutting out the designs. Load your vinyl on to your mat.

3 Remember if using Smart Materials to change the setting, otherwise the system may get confused that the materials are not on a mat.

4 Trim your vinyl back as you go, keeping just a small amount around the designs. Keep any spare small scraps of vinyl for future projects.

5 Now you are ready to weed your designs. The Joy Xtra comes with a small weeder which is useful for really fine, fiddly pieces. Or, use your weeder – whichever you have and/or prefer. Weed away all excess areas of vinyl away from your designs.

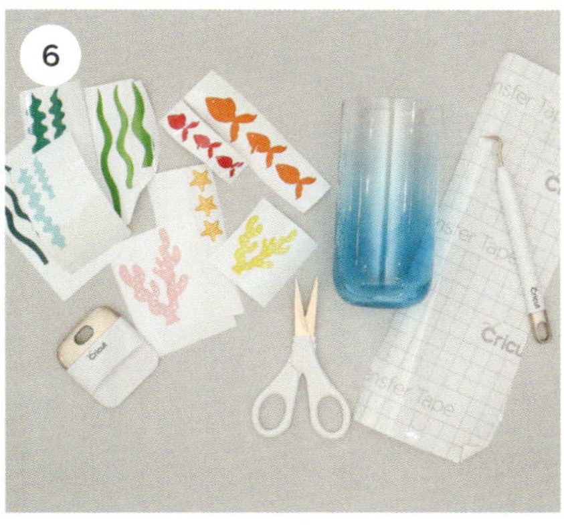

6 You are now ready to start adding your designs to the tumbler. Make sure your tumbler is nice and clean, dry and dust free.

7 Cut a small piece of Transfer Tape. Remember, you can use this several times, so try to use this one piece for the whole project.

8 Peel back the tape from the liner.

9 Place on to your design. Use your scraper tool to gently but firmly push your design down on to your tape. You can do this both front and back if it helps to move your design from the liner on to the tape. It helps to do this against a hard surface such as a smooth, flat table.

10 Peel away the white liner to reveal the design on your tape.

11 Place the design on to the glass wherever you would like.

13 Smooth out to ensure there are no air bubbles trapped underneath.

14 Gently peel away the Transfer Tape, leaving your design on the glass.

15 Move on to the other part of your designs, cutting them out from the carrier sheets where necessary. For some of the simpler shapes, you could peel off instead of using the tape.

16 You can layer the vinyls on top of each other, but try not to have more than 3 or 4 layers together as it will become too thick.

17 Work your way round the glass, adding the corals, seaweed, starfish and fish wherever you would like.

18 And you are done! A lovely underwater-themed toothbrush holder.

NOTE Wait for 24–48 hours before contact with water to allow the vinyl to be fully fixed into position. I would recommend hand washing this only.

GOING BEYOND THE MAKE

These fish and seaweed designs don't need to be just used in bathroom creations! I saw this blue, bubble-filled serving bowl and thought it would be a perfect combination. This would make a beautiful, fun fruit bowl, or for serving salad perhaps. I have cut the designs out twice and made one set slightly larger. The benefit of using SVG files is they can be adapted to be bigger or smaller, used in many ways and created in multiple materials. These fish and coral designs would make a fabulous edge to a T-shirt or skirt using iron-on.

SUNFLOWER
SEEDS
PUMPKIN
SEEDS
CHILLI
POWDER
ALMONDS
SMOKED
PAPRIKA
RAISINS

Storage Jars

I feel like Cricut machines were absolutely born for organization. When I got my first cutting machine I wanted to label everything! The toy boxes in the playroom, the boxes in the garage and every jar or container possible in our kitchen. This is a quick project that is so effective and useful. These glass jars are slightly larger than your classic spice jars and would also be useful for storing nuts, seeds or dried fruit.

YOU WILL NEED

MACHINE

- Cricut Machine and Blade (I used Cricut Joy and Fine Point Blade for Cricut Joy)

TOOLS

- Cricut Weeder
- Cricut Scissors
- Cricut Scraper
- Cricut Spatula (optional)
- Cricut StandardGrip Mat (if required)

MATERIALS

- Cricut Permanent Vinyl in your choice of colours
- Cricut Transfer Tape
- Glass or Plastic Jars

FONT

- Baylac

NOTES

- I have chosen to use Smart Vinyl, but please use a Cricut StandardGrip Mat if you are using small scraps or standard vinyls.
- I have chosen the Baylac font as it is nice and clear, yet slightly quirky! It is important in organization to choose a crisp, clean font so everything is easy to visually process.

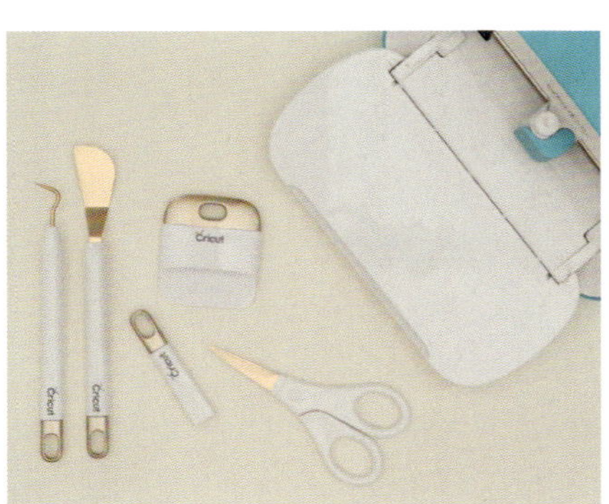

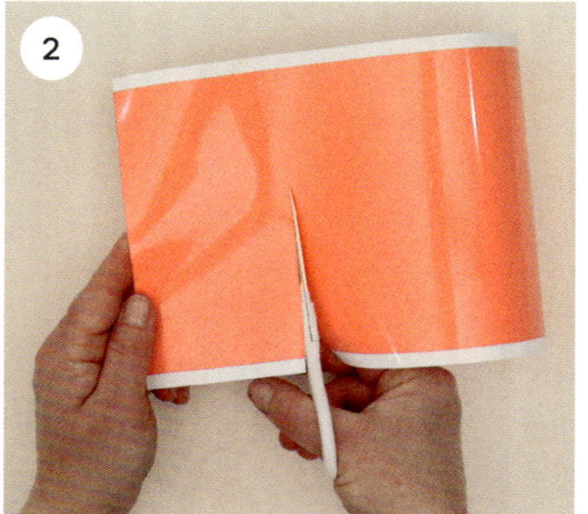

1 Open Design Space and type the text you require for your labels onto your Canvas. I have made each label around ½in (1.2cm) tall to suit the size of these jars. Follow the on-screen instructions to cut your text, loading any different coloured vinyls as required.

2 Where required, trim your cut text from the roll or any larger sheets of vinyl.

3 Make sure to save any smaller vinyl pieces for another project. I have kept these for the Confetti Artwork project on page 32.

4 Weed any excess vinyl away from your text using your weeder.

5 The weeding tool is particularly good for fiddly pieces, such as getting small parts of vinyl out from letter centres.

6 Cut each word or phrase out, so they are all separate.

7 Cut a piece of Transfer Tape for the size required.

8 Peel the tape away from the carrier sheet and place your Transfer Tape on to one of your cut-out words or phrases.

9 Use your scraper to push your design on to the tape.

10 Pull your design away from the carrier sheet.

11 Place your text on to the jar. I like to use the lines on the Transfer Tape as a guide to help me line things up where I would like.

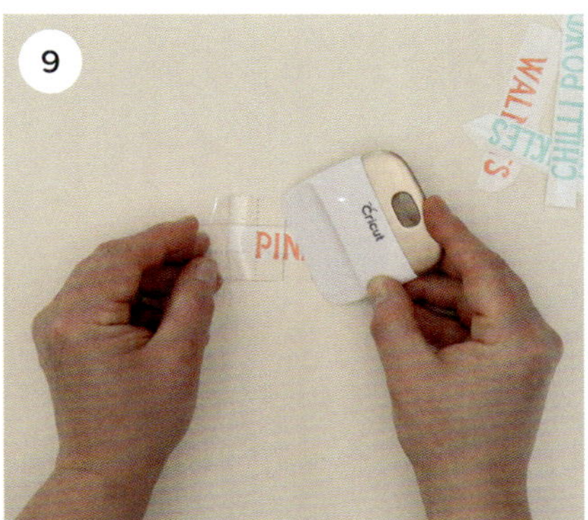

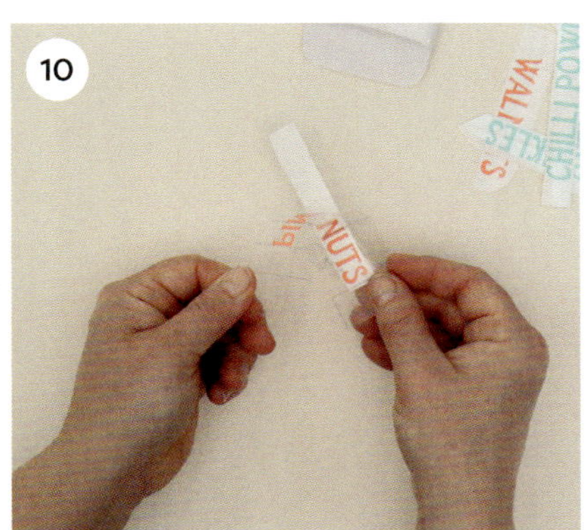

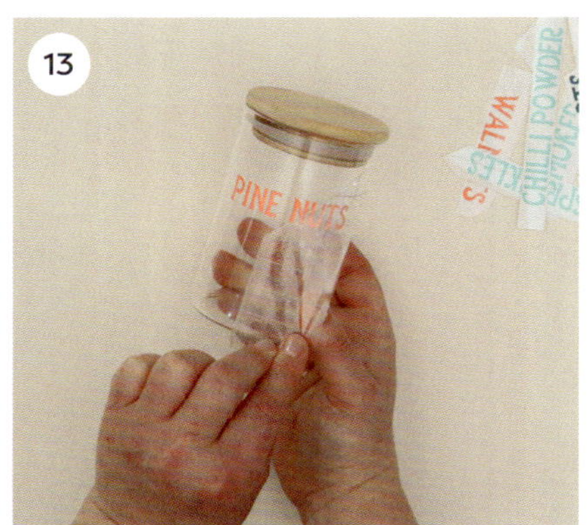

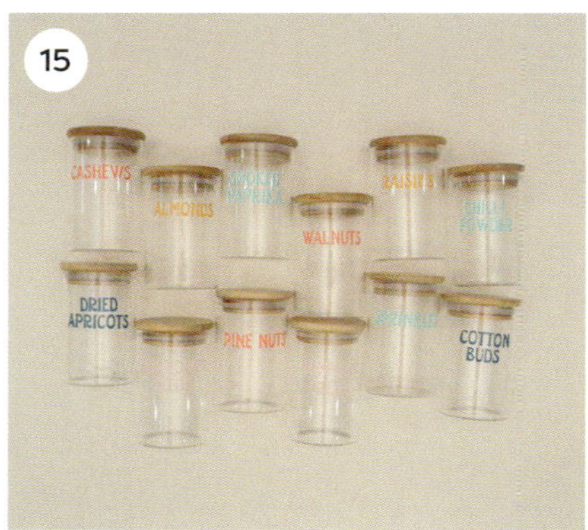

12 Use your thumbs to gently push your design on to the glass, making sure to push out any air bubbles.

13 Pull the tape away from your design, leaving everything in position.

14 If required, you can split some of the names and place them one under the other.

15 Repeat with your other jars. Make sure they are clean before you add any food. However, wait 24-48 hours before there is any contact with water if you do need to clean them as this allows the vinyl to be fully fixed. I would recommend hand washing these only.

16 These jars don't just need to be useful in the kitchen, I have also labelled one for use in our bathroom.

GOING BEYOND THE MAKE

You could make the labels as simple or complex as you like – adding borders, additional decorative details or shapes. You can also create labels using the 'draw' function (see the Jam Jars project on page 36).

Noah
Florence
Evie
Harriet

Children's Tableware Set

This colourful and personalized tableware set is not only perfect for everyday home use, it's also great for a children's party. This could even be a good children's party activity – it then becomes the party bag, with each child having their own cup, bowl, plate and spoon to take home.

YOU WILL NEED

MACHINE

- Cricut Machine and Blade (I used Cricut Joy and Fine Point Blade for Cricut Joy)

TOOLS

- Cricut Weeder
- Cricut Scissors
- Cricut Scraper
- Cricut Spatula (optional)
- Cricut StandardGrip Mat (if not using Smart Vinyl)

MATERIALS

- Cricut Permanent Vinyl in your choice of colours
- Cricut Transfer Tape
- Cups, Bowls, Plates, Spoons

IMAGES

- Exclusive Butterfly SVG
- Exclusive Small Flower SVG

FONT

- Watercolour Brush Script

NOTES

- I would recommend washing these by hand. Allow 24 hours after application before allowing contact with water to ensure the vinyl glue has fully adhered.
- Don't place your vinyl shapes inside a bowl, on a plate main surface, on the spoon bowl, or too near or on the very edge of your cup rim to minimize contact with food and your mouth while eating and drinking.
- This project is aimed at older children and not babies or young children.
- If you are using Smart Vinyl, you will not require the use of a mat.

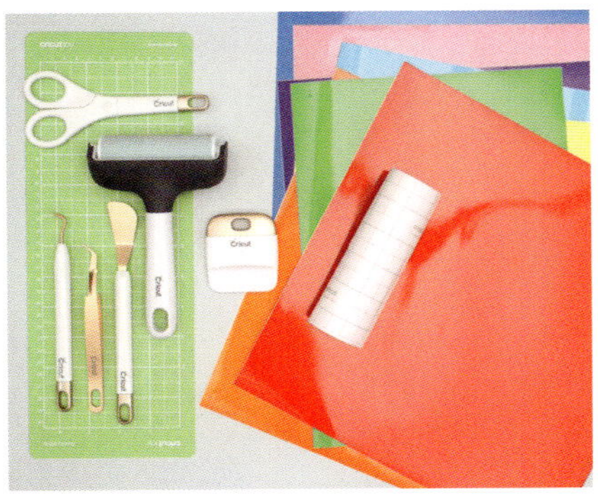

1 Open Design Space and choose your font before typing the names you require. Upload the exclusive Butterfly SVG and Small Flower SVG files. I have duplicated the butterfly and flower shapes several times (around 15) on the Canvas to allow plenty of stickers to add to all of the blank items. Trim your vinyl if required and add to your mat or load your Smart Materials. Follow the on-screen instructions for cutting.

2 Use your brayer to smooth out your vinyl. You can see small particles in the glossy vinyl that will be stuck to the mat underneath. These won't impact your cut if your vinyl is firmly in position. But do try to get out any larger air bubbles with your brayer.

3 Once cut, weed away your designs using your weeder. Repeat the cuts with any other colours.

4 Trim the cut-out names. You will use Transfer Tape to transfer these. Cut a small piece of tape that is big enough to cover the name.

5 Use your scraper to push the name on to the Transfer Tape.

6 Pull the name away from the carrier sheet. Don't forget you can reuse this piece of tape for the next name. Place the name on to the cup. Try to use the top of the cup as a guide to line things up. These specific cups also have small linear ridges, which is helpful. Use your thumbs to gently push your design on to the cup, making sure to push out any air bubbles.

1

2

3

4

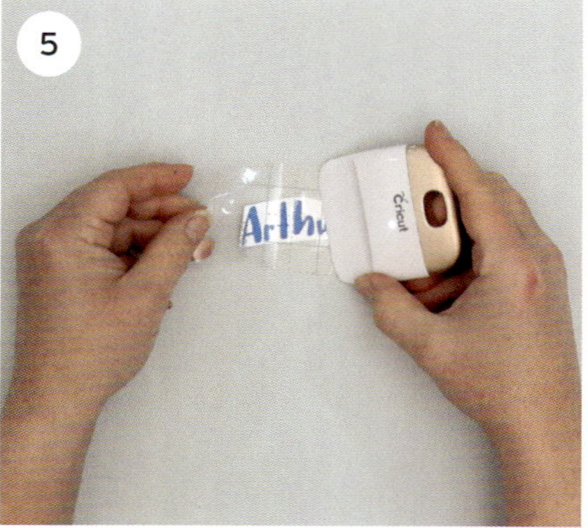
5

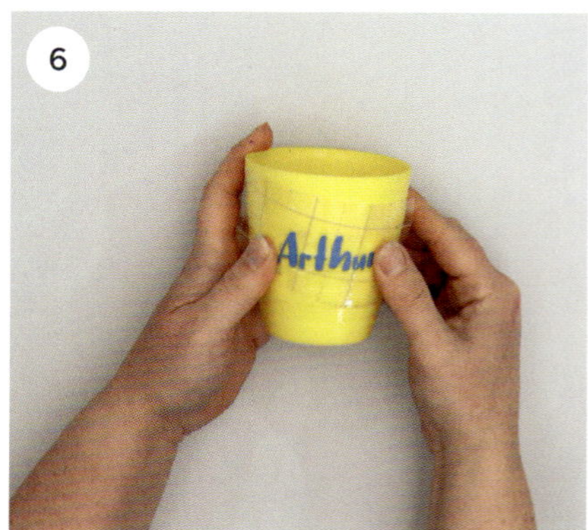
6

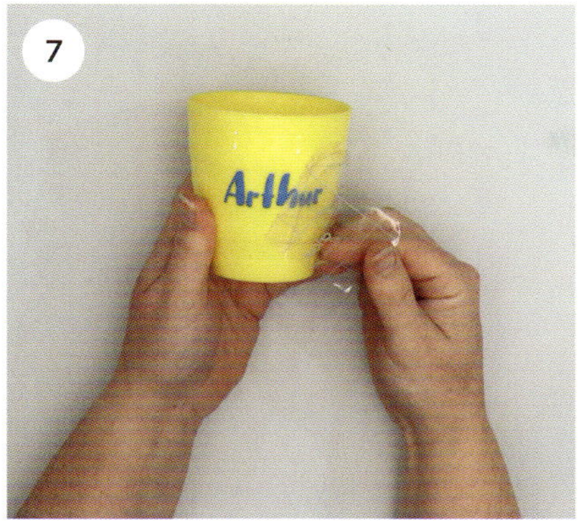

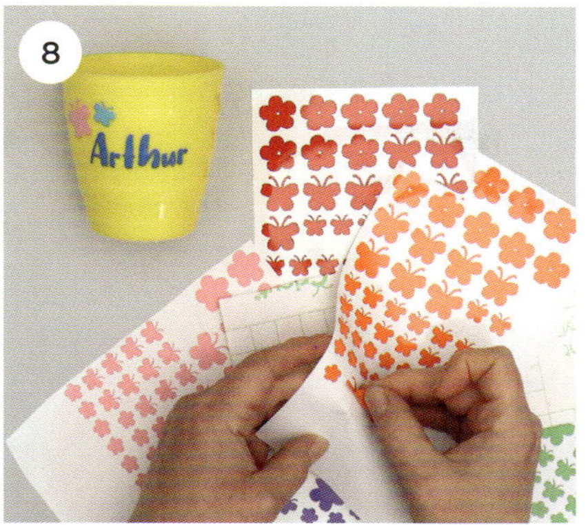

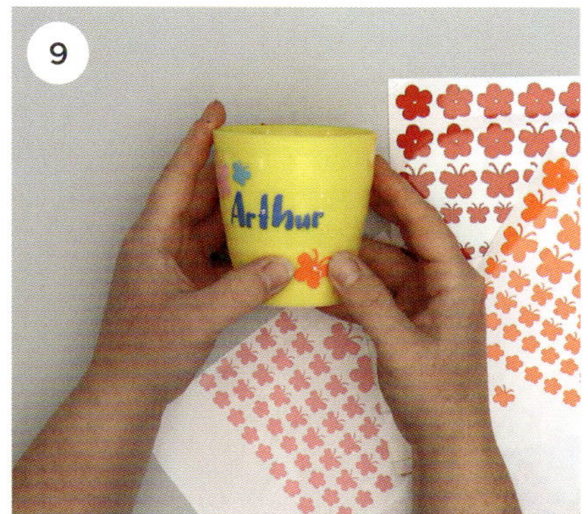

7 Pull the tape away from your name. Repeat with the other cups and any other names.

8 Peel the rest of the shapes from the carrier sheet like 'stickers'. Use your tweezers if this helps. I find bending the carrier sheet can also help you remove the shapes.

9 Place the shapes wherever you like around the name. You could keep them all the same colour and design or mix and match for a multi-coloured effect.

10 Keep adding the shapes until you are happy with your finished cup. Repeat with your other cups.

11 Repeat the sticker shapes on the other items. Just add the butterfly and flower shapes around the edge of the plates, on the bowl sides and on the spoon handle. You could also add the child's name on every item too if you like.

12 And you are done! One bright tableware set.

GOING BEYOND THE MAKE

Making children's personalized items is super easy with Cricut vinyl and iron-on. You could cut out and make children's names or initials for clothing, bags – even cushions and bedding. I like to cut out my children's initials in iron-on for labelling inside their school uniform and in vinyl for their water bottles and lunchboxes.

Space Mug

Using heat-activated, colour-changing vinyl makes for a truly out-of-this world effect on this humble blue mug. I chose a 'reactive' glaze mug for depth within the blue colour, reminiscent of the dark night sky. These purple planets and galaxy swirls will change colour to turquoise as you make your hot cuppa, before changing back again as it cools, which is just incredibly fun and crafty magic!

YOU WILL NEED

MACHINE

- [ ] Cricut Machine and Blade (I used Cricut Explore 3 and Fine Point Blade for Cricut Explore)

TOOLS

- [ ] Cricut StandardGrip Mat
- [ ] Cricut Brayer
- [ ] Cricut Scraper
- [ ] Cricut Weeder
- [ ] Cricut Scissors
- [ ] Cricut Spatula (optional)
- [ ] Cricut Tweezers (optional)

MATERIALS

- [ ] Cricut Permanent Vinyl in your choice of colours (I have used pink, aqua, gold and silver)
- [ ] Cricut Heat-Activated, Colour-Changing Vinyl (Purple/Turquoise)
- [ ] Cricut Transfer Tape
- [ ] Mug

IMAGES

- [ ] Exclusive Space SVG

NOTES

- Did you know Cricut also have offer a Cold-Activated Colour-Changing Vinyl? This could look lovely on a water bottle or glass.

- This design could, of course, also be made in standard Permanent Vinyl without the colour change option to utilize materials you may already have.

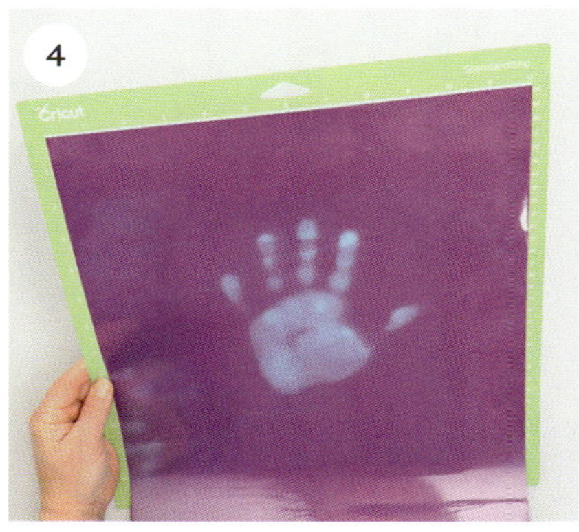

1 It is useful to measure around your mug so you can adjust the SVG file in Design Space should you need to. This mug was around 9in (23cm) from handle to handle.

2 Upload the Space SVG file and add to your Design Space Canvas. Add your vinyl to your mat and use your brayer to make sure everything is stuck down smoothly and is free of air bubbles.

3 Follow the on-screen instructions for cutting the design. Load the mat and materials when requested.

4 You will find that your heat-activated vinyl will start changing colour as you touch and use it from your own body warmth.

5 Once your designs have been cut, trim them out from your vinyl and reserve any spare for future projects.

6 Weed any excess vinyl away from your designs using your weeder.

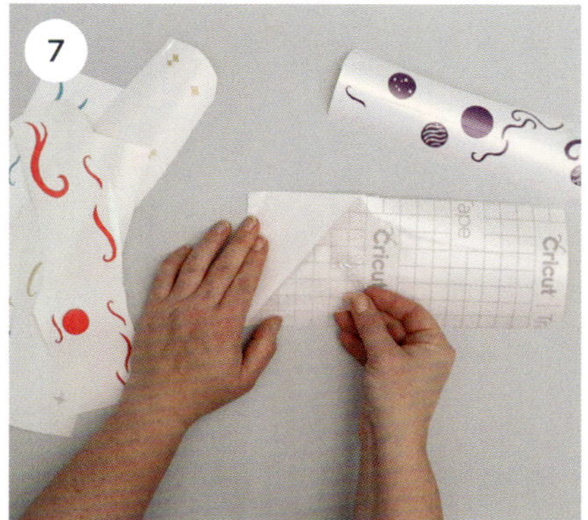

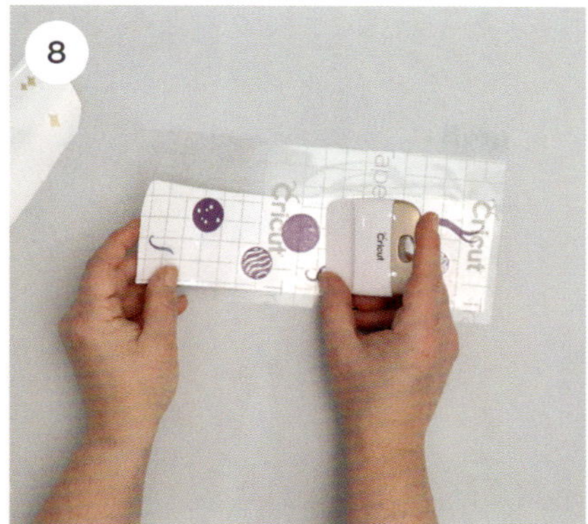

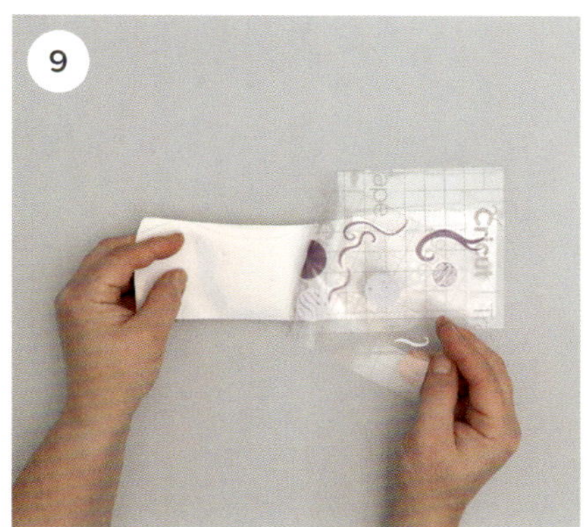

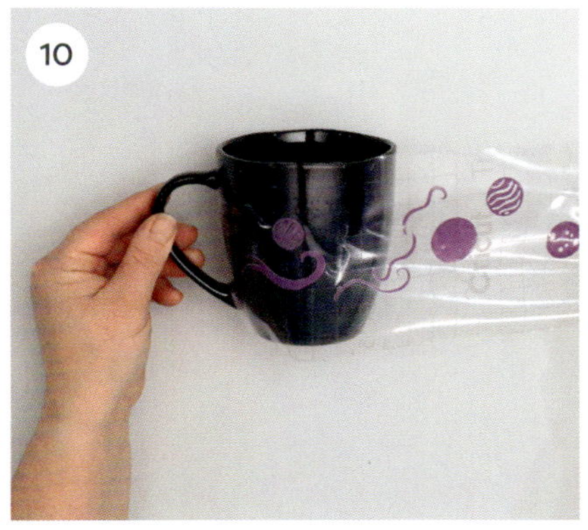

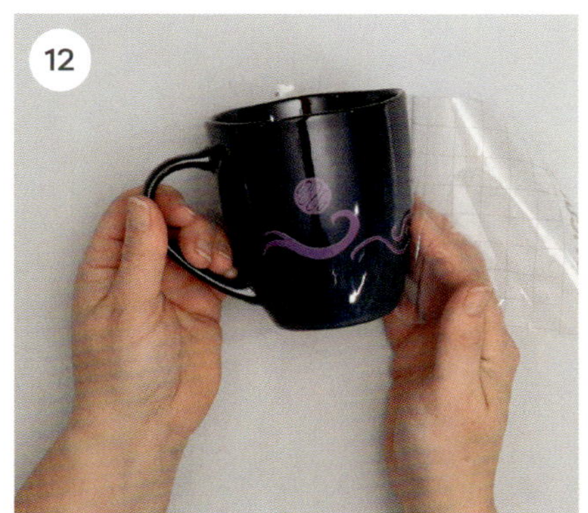

7 Cut out a piece of Transfer Tape that is bigger than your design. Peel the tape away from its carrier sheet.

8 Apply the tape to one of your layers. Begin with your heat-activated vinyl layer as some of the other colours, such as the gold planet ring, layer on to this. Use your scraper to gently push the tape down on to your design. You can turn it over and repeat if you feel it needs extra pressure to transfer.

9 Peel back your tape with the design attached.

10 Starting from one handle, apply the design around your mug.

11 The mug I have chosen is slightly narrower at the base than the top, which affects the angle of how the design transfers. If your mug is a similar shape, without straight sides, you may see that the Transfer Tape buckles and folds in places. Don't worry, just try to apply the design all the way around, as centrally as possible.

12 Peel back your Transfer Tape, making sure everything is firmly attached to the mug.

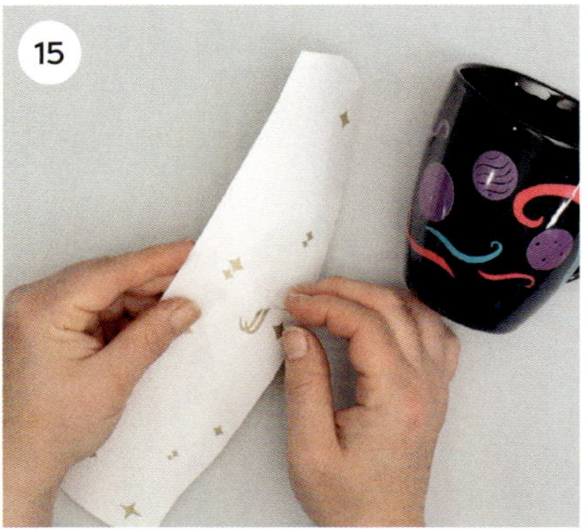

14 Now add on your second layer. You may find with a diagonal form of mug, everything doesn't quite line up exactly as you hoped. That is OK! This Space design wasn't meant to be exact, but you can also transfer each piece at a time if needed. Just gently push the Transfer Tape where you want your vinyl to be before moving on to the next piece. If you prefer, you could trim out each piece of vinyl before transferring separately. You can use the design on your Canvas in Design Space as your visual guide.

15 With the gold and silver stars and planet rings, I found it much easier to peel off and add without the tape. The texture of the gold and silver permanent vinyl doesn't always adhere to standard Transfer Tape (you may need StrongGrip). Equally, the stars just fit nicely in around the planets and galaxies, so feel free to just add them wherever you like.

16 And you are done! One magic, colour-changing mug, ready for you to enjoy your favourite cuppa. Mine is a green tea! Make sure you wait 24–48 hours before contact with water. This allows the vinyl to be fully fixed. Heat-Activated, Colour-Changing Vinyl is handwash only.

GOING BEYOND THE MAKE

You could easily adapt this design to add a personalized name on the mug: there are gaps that could allow for this or you can just move any vinyl pieces out of the way. This space design could also be made much larger and turned into a wall decal, perhaps. My son's room is heavily space themed and if I made this design in a holographic or textured vinyl it would certainly make a fabulously fun mural! The individual elements would also look fabulous on clothing. Choose dark fabrics and bright iron-ons for a stand-out magic design feature.

Boats Tea Towel

I just love a funky tea towel. They brighten up the kitchen and give a lift to the ongoing chore of washing up. Tea towels also make lovely gifts. I have been known to wrap many a recipe book in a beautiful tea towel as the 'gift wrap'. My parents live on the Isle of Wight and this crinkly soft blue linen reminds me of the gentle sea. The classically nautical red, white and blue colours are very reminiscent of Cowes Week yachts!

YOU WILL NEED

MACHINES

- Cricut Machine and Blade (I used Cricut Explore 3 and Fine Point Blade for Cricut Explore)
- Cricut EasyPress

TOOLS

- Cricut StandardGrip Mat
- Cricut Weeder
- Cricut Scissors
- Cricut Brayer
- Cricut Spatula (optional)
- Cricut EasyPress Mat

MATERIALS

- Cricut Everyday Iron-On in your choice of colours (I have used a selection of blues, red, white and grey)
- 100% Cotton Tea Towel

IMAGES

- Design Space Boat SVG #M490637EA
- Design Space Boat SVG #M4905E58A

NOTE

- While I am using my two boats images in Design Space for this project, you could of course use this technique with whatever images you like.
- While I have repeated the boats across the whole tea towel, you could also do a little row of them just at one end if you prefer.
- If you are using Smart iron-on you will not require the use of a mat.

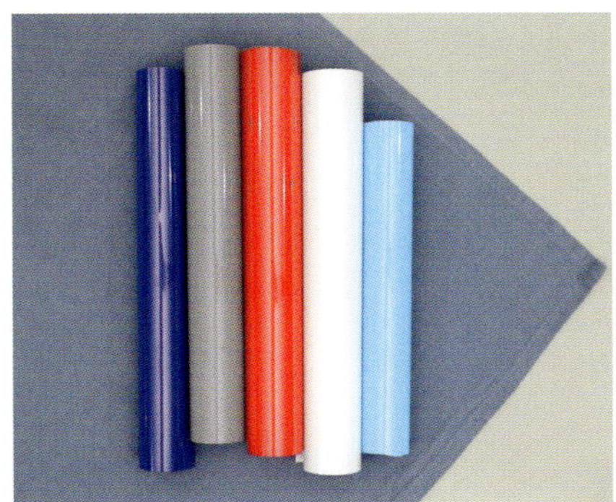

1 Open Design Space and access the Boats SVGs. Following the instructions on screen, add the relevant materials onto your mat and use your brayer to ensure they are free of creases and air bubbles. Alternatively load your Smart Materials directly into the machine.

2 Make sure your materials are sized correctly for the machine you are using. Remember to attach your iron-on with the shiny carrier sheet side face-down and the matte iron-on face-up. I have cut 6 of the small boat trio (#M490637EA) and 3 of the larger boat (#M4905E58A).

NOTE Most iron-on designs require you to make sure you use the 'Mirror' function but, as these look almost the same both ways around, this does not need to be activated.

3 Trim back the iron-on around your cut designs and keep any spare for future smaller projects. It can sometimes be hard to see where the cut lines are. If you turn towards a light (or use a BrightPad) this can help.

4 Using your weeder, weed out your designs.

5 Cut out each element of your design, ready for attaching on to your tea towel. Repeat with the other colours.

6 I find it best to group the different types of shapes/colours together.

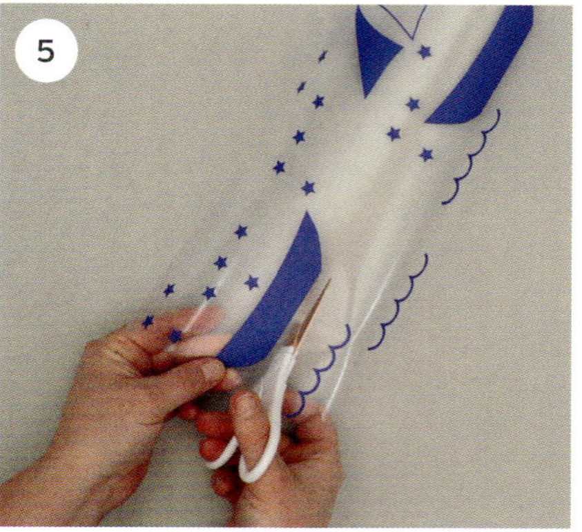

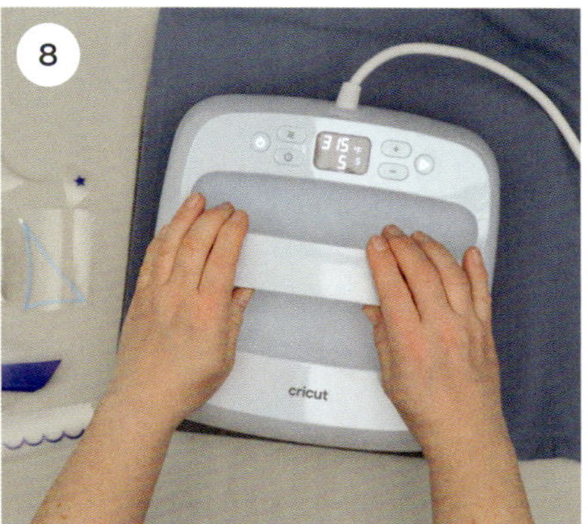

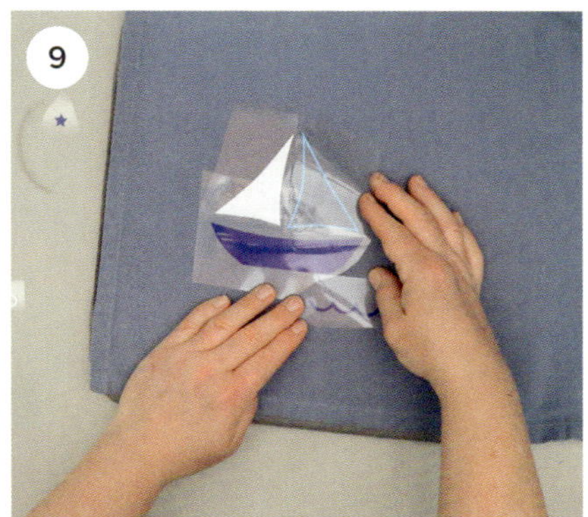

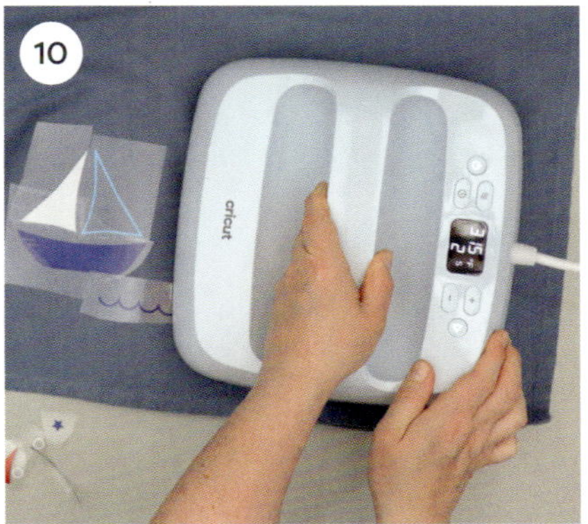

7 Turn on your EasyPress as it will need a small amount of time to heat up. Check the Cricut Heat Guide for the latest advice on what temperature and time settings are recommended for your chosen materials and your EasyPress version. Check to see if your tea towel has a hook, so you can make sure your design is the correct way up.

8 Following the heat guide recommendations, pre-heat your cotton tea towel blank.

9 Make sure all of your design is fully covered with pieces of the thick, clear carrier sheet. Following the heat guide, use your EasyPress to attach the iron-on to your tea towel.

10 Add the next pieces of design and move your EasyPress across to press your design. The EasyPress is heated uniformly across the entire hot plate, so it will work exactly the same in whichever direction you apply it downwards. Use it whichever way is most appropriate for your plug direction (as I have done in the photo) to make sure the wire doesn't get trapped underneath.

11 If you want to layer up your design, wait until your pressed iron-on is cool before gently peeling back your carrier sheet pieces. If the iron-on hasn't completely stuck at this stage, reheat it as per the instructions before peeling back again.

12 Trim down your second layer pieces before adding.

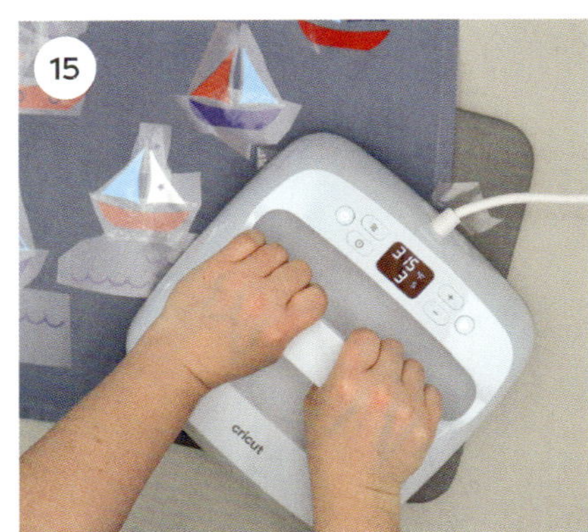

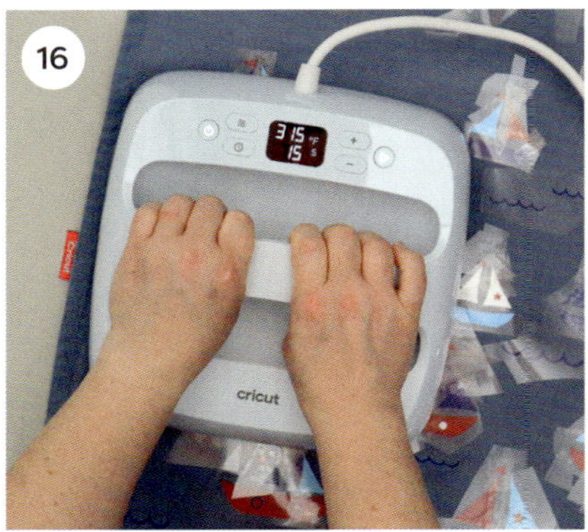

13 Make sure to cover all parts of iron-on with carrier sheet pieces again.

14 Continue following the same heat instructions to adhere the second layer of iron-on.

15 Continue adding your boats across the tea towel. Continue adding and layering up your designs so you have your boats, sea and stars.

16 With a multi-image and multilayer design such as this, I like to cover everything in a carrier sheet and give everything one final press.

17 Once everything is cool, peel back your carrier sheets to reveal the design. Continue peeling everything back and checking to ensure all layers of iron-on are attached.

18 And you are finished! One beautiful tea towel to make you smile when washing up!

GOING BEYOND THE MAKE

Tea towels make an excellent source of good-quality fabric. You could turn this idea into a cute nautical-themed pillow or cut one up to make some sort of patchwork. This boat design would also work well on the Lunchbox idea on page 130 or perhaps recreated in Infusible Ink for the Ceramic Coasters on page 102.

Citrus Table Setting

This vibrant citrus design makes for a fresh and beautiful table setting, perfect for summer lunches or to brighten darker evenings! The soft, pale linen fabric contrasts with, and highlights, the warm fruits and lush foliage. The napkins, with their simple layout of just one fruit, a slice and the leaves, complement the full citrus runner. This would make a beautiful housewarming gift.

YOU WILL NEED

MACHINES

- Cricut Machine and Blade (I used Maker 3 and Fine Point Blade for Cricut Maker)
- Cricut EasyPress

TOOLS

- Cricut StandardGrip Mat
- Cricut Weeder
- Cricut Scissors
- Cricut Brayer
- Cricut Spatula (optional)
- Cricut Tweezers (optional)
- Cricut Scraper (optional)
- Cricut EasyPress Mat

MATERIALS

- Cricut Everyday Iron-On in your choice of colours (I have used a selection of oranges, yellows and greens)
- 100% Cotton Linen Table Runner and Napkins

IMAGES

- Exclusive Oranges and Lemons SVG

NOTES

- Most iron-on designs require you to make sure you use the 'Mirror' function but, as these look almost the same both ways around, this does not need to be activated.
- If you are using Smart iron-on you will not require the use of a mat.

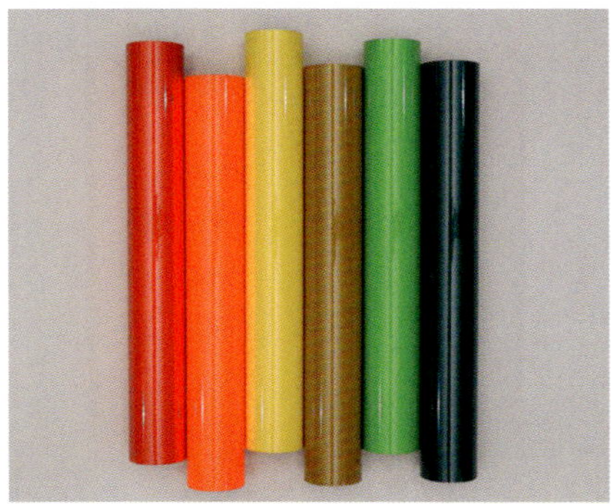

1 Upload the exclusive Oranges and Lemons SVG files to Design Space. Attach your iron-on to your mat using the brayer to ensure everything is smooth and free of air bubbles. Remember to attach your iron-on with the shiny carrier sheet face-down – you want the matte iron-on to be face-up. Alternatively, load your Smart Materials directly into your machine.

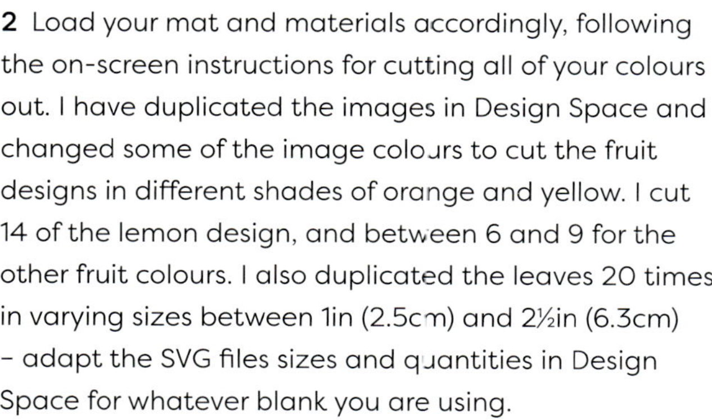

2 Load your mat and materials accordingly, following the on-screen instructions for cutting all of your colours out. I have duplicated the images in Design Space and changed some of the image colours to cut the fruit designs in different shades of orange and yellow. I cut 14 of the lemon design, and between 6 and 9 for the other fruit colours. I also duplicated the leaves 20 times in varying sizes between 1in (2.5cm) and 2½in (6.3cm) – adapt the SVG files sizes and quantities in Design Space for whatever blank you are using.

3 Using your weeder, weed out your designs.

4 Repeat with your other colours.

5 Once your designs are fully weeded, cut out each element of your design, ready for attaching on to your napkins and runner.

6 I find it best to group the different types of shapes/colours together.

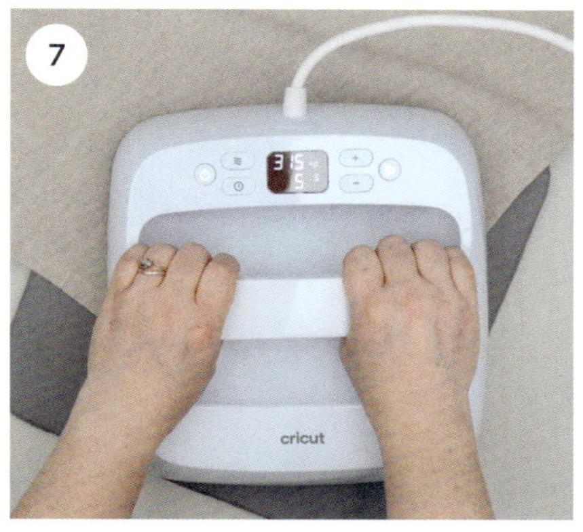
7

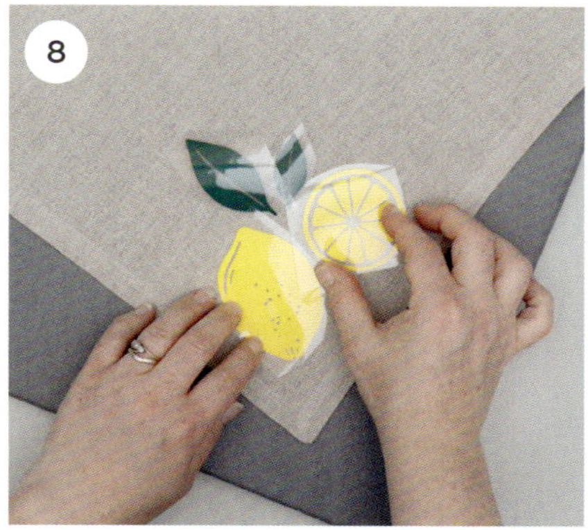
8

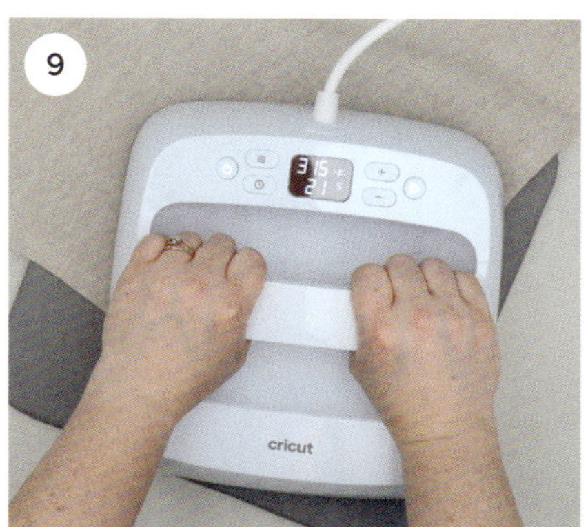
9

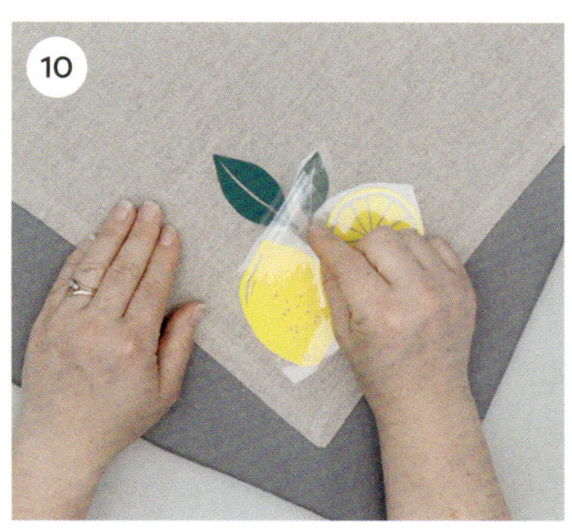
10

11

12

7 Turn on your EasyPress ready for making, as it will need a small amount of time to heat up. Check the Cricut Heat Guide for latest advice on what temperature and time settings are recommended for your chosen materials and your EasyPress version. Following the heat guide recommendations, pre-heat one of your napkin blanks.

8 Lay your design where you would like on the napkin. I have chosen to do a corner of each napkin with one piece of fruit, one slice of fruit and a couple of leaves. You could of course do more, or less – whatever you would like! Be careful as the napkin will of course be slightly hot from the pre-heating.

9 Following the heat guide, use your EasyPress to attach the iron-on to your napkin.

10 Once everything is cool, peel back your carrier sheet to reveal the design.

11 Continue peeling back your design, and if anything hasn't 100% adhered to your blank, you can always cover it with any carrier sheets and repeat the heating.

12 One napkin, done!

13 Repeat the same process with your other napkins.

14 I have a set of four napkins and chose to mix and match each napkin to have different citrus fruits. I chose two lemons and two different-coloured oranges.

15 It is the same process here on the runner as it is for the napkins, but with much more condensed fruits and leaves. The design is concentrated down the centre of the runner. As the pieces are so close together, I have had to heat everything in stages. Keep the carrier sheet over each piece to protect the iron-on surface from damage. Try to make sure as well that any carrier sheet doesn't become trapped under any iron-on.

16 Peel back the carrier sheet pieces, checking that everything is attached to the fabric securely.

17 Sometimes, you need slightly more heat, so repeat where necessary, if required. Once again, make sure to cover anything that will come into direct contact with the EasyPress surface.

18 And you are finished! One beautiful tableware set full of citrussy, vibrant colours.

GOING BEYOND THE MAKE

These citrus designs would look lovely on any coordinating tableware, such as the Fiesta Table Mats on page 76. Or cut them out in vinyl and add to tumblers or a serving jug for fruity summer drinks! The fruits could also easily work in Infusible Ink on the Ceramic Coasters on page 102.

Fiesta Table Mats

Did you know that you can add iron-on to cork? It applies really easily. This bright table mat and coaster project coordinates Everyday and Metallic Iron-On. I just love how the vibrant and shimmering colours contrast against the more neutral cork texture. These would certainly brighten up any table setting.

YOU WILL NEED

MACHINES

- Cricut Machine and Blade (I used Cricut Joy Xtra and Cricut Joy Xtra FIne-Point Blade)
- Cricut EasyPress

TOOLS

- Cricut Joy Xtra StandardGrip Mat (if required)
- Cricut Weeder
- Cricut Scissors
- Cricut Brayer
- Cricut Scraper
- Cricut Spatula
- Cricut Tweezers (optional)
- Cricut EasyPress Mat

CRICUT MATERIALS

- Cricut Everyday Iron-On in your choice of colours
- Cricut Metallic Iron-On in your choice of colours (I have used two coordinating colours for the mat and coaster set)
- Cork Table Mats and Coasters

IMAGES

- Design Space Basic Free Triangle Shape

NOTES

- This make is available as a saved 'Project' through my Design Space profile if you would like to replicate or customize it. See the instructions on page 80 if you want to make it yourself from scratch.

- Please make sure you keep your EasyPress on the recommended storage plate when switched on: it can get extremely hot! Use your EasyPress to create this project on a flat surface.

1 Trim and attach your iron-on to your mat using the brayer to ensure everything is smooth and free of air bubbles. Remember to attach your iron-on with the shiny carrier sheet side face-down – you want the matte iron-on to be face-up. Alternatively, load your Smart Materials directly into your machine.

NOTE: Most iron-on designs require you to make sure you use the 'Mirror' function but, as these are the same both ways round, this does not need to be activated.

2 Load your materials accordingly, following the on-screen instructions for cutting out all of your colours.

3 Peel your iron-on from the mat.

4 Trim back the iron-on around your designs and keep any spare for future smaller projects. It can sometimes be hard to see where the cut lines are, if you turn towards a light (or use a CricutBright Pad) this can help.

5 Weed out your design, using your weeder.

6 Cut out each strip of triangles so they are ready to apply on to your cork mats.

7 Turn on your EasyPress. It will need a small amount of time to heat up. Check the Cricut Heat Guide for the latest advice on what temperature and time settings are recommended for your chosen materials and your EasyPress model.

8 Place your design where you would like it to be on your cork mat. The carrier sheet should be slightly sticky to help with this.

9 Following the heat-guide recommendations, use your EasyPress to attach the iron-on to your cork mat. The EasyPress is heated uniformly across the entire hot plate, so it will work exactly the same in whichever direction you apply it downwards. Use it whichever way is most appropriate for your plug direction to ensure the main wire stays away from being trapped underneath. Your EasyPress may be smaller than your design. You will need to complete the pressing in stages, moving across to repeat.

10 Move your EasyPress across, if required, to complete the pressing of your design.

11 You will need to leave your now attached iron-on to cool down before removing the liner, so turn your cork mat around and repeat steps 8–10 for the other side.

12 Repeat with your EasyPress.

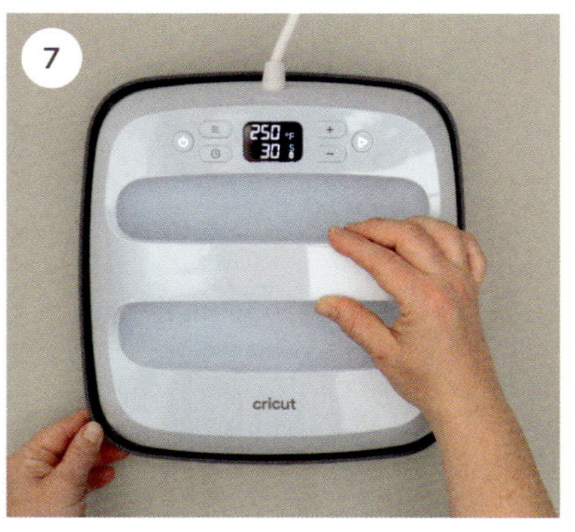

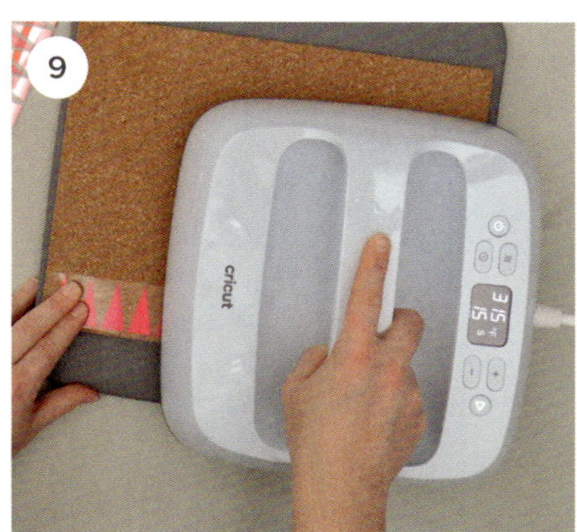

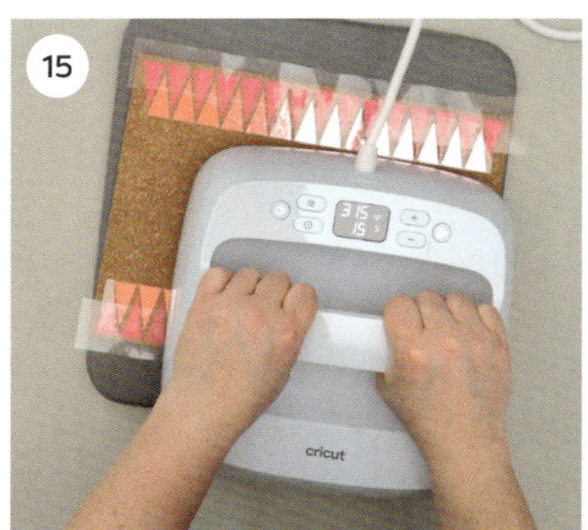

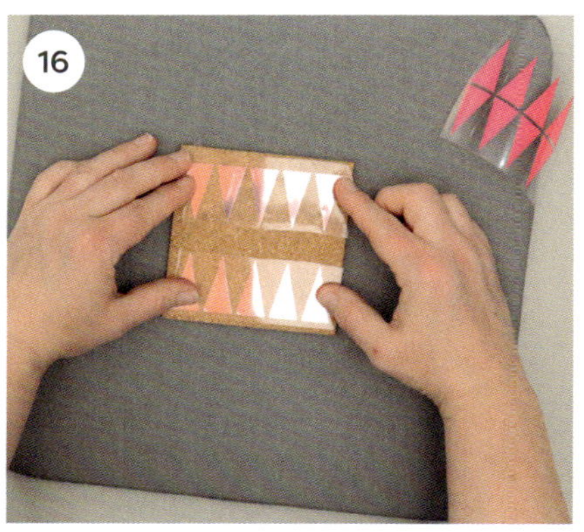

13 Once completely cool, peel back your liner.

14 Now position your metallic strip of triangles. I have left a small gap between each row, creating a small zig-zag of cork between each colour.

15 Again, using the heat guide instructions as a guide, use your EasyPress to apply the metallic triangles.

NOTE You need to ensure your already applied iron-on is covered by its carrier strip so it does not come into direct contact with the EasyPress hot plate or the iron-on surface could become damaged.

16 Repeat this process with the coasters.

17 Repeat with your other mats, coasters and colours to complete. And you are done. One vibrant, colourful fiesta set!

HOW TO MAKE FROM SCRATCH

Add the triangle shape to your Canvas in Design Space. I measured my table mats and coasters to calculate how many and what size triangles I would need and duplicated the shape accordingly. I used 58 triangles in total per table mat and 18 per coaster. These were split into rows:

2 x 15 (Everyday) and 2 x 14 (Metallic) per mat
2 x 5 (Metallic) and 2 x 4 (Everyday) per coaster

You may need more or less, depending on the size of your own cork mats and coasters. To make the triangles sit in a straight line, I have used the 'Align' and 'Distribute Evenly' functions. To cut the triangles as they appear in their rows I used the 'Attach' function.

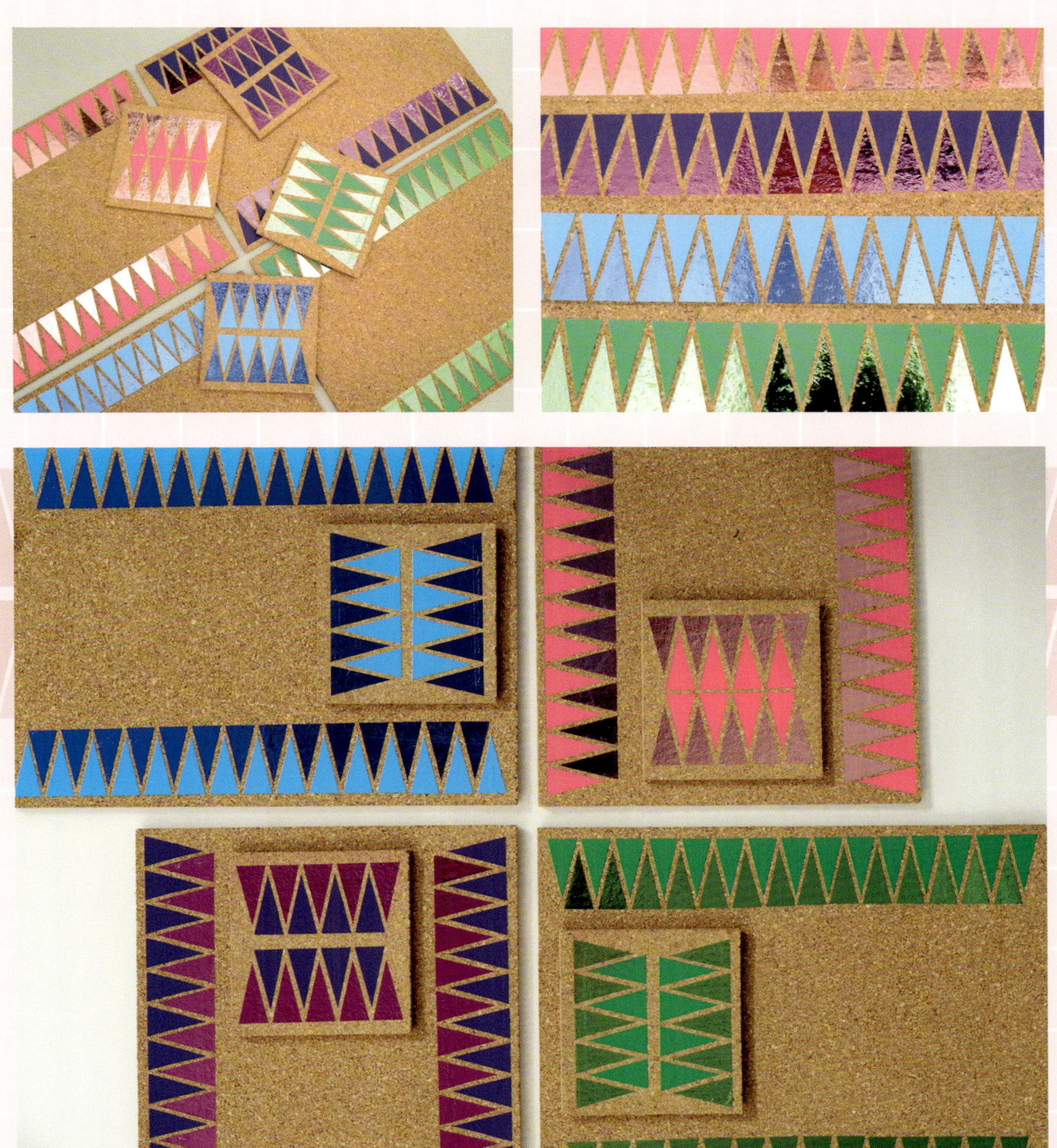

GOING BEYOND THE MAKE

You could create similar designs with other free shapes too, such as repeating squares or perhaps overlapping circles. This repeating triangle pattern would also look lovely on a table runner, cushions, or even the edge of a shirt or skirt!

HOME
STUDIO

Faux Leather Keyring

This simple but truly effective project makes me want to make keyrings for every key we have and for everyone I know. This quick make would be fabulous for little personalized gifts. It amazes me that the little Cricut Joy can cut faux leather with its standard fine-point blade. I have chosen the Cricut brown faux leather, alongside the rose gold iron-on, but you could easily experiment with all sorts of colour combinations.

YOU WILL NEED

MACHINES

- Cricut Machine and Blade (I used Cricut Joy and Fine Point Blade for Cricut Joy)
- Cricut EasyPress Mini

TOOLS

- Cricut StandardGrip Mat
- Cricut Weeder
- Cricut Scissors
- Cricut Brayer
- Cricut Spatula
- Cricut Scraper (optional)
- Cricut EasyPress Mat
- Glue Gun

MATERIALS

- Cricut Rose Gold Foil Iron-On (or your choice of colour)
- Cricut Faux Leather (Paper-Thin)
- Metal Keyring Loop(s)

IMAGES

- Exclusive Keyring SVG

FONT

- Cricut Sans

NOTES

- The Cricut Sans font is the classic font that Design Space always defaults to, but I find it a really clear, precise choice, particularly for labelling. You can choose whichever font you like but make sure you use a font size smaller than the keyring outline.
- This project could be made with any EasyPress machine, but the Mini does make for a more precise transfer.
- I have chosen to use a hot glue gun. Other glues may work, but be sure to test them on a small piece of scrap leather before proceeding with the main project.

1 Upload the exclusive Keyring SVG file and write your text in your choice of font on your Canvas in Design Space. I have duplicated the Keyring SVG for making two keyrings. Trim your faux leather to fit on your mat.

2 Your faux leather needs to be cut face-down. Use your brayer to make sure the faux leather is firmly attached and is free of air bubbles.

3 Follow the on-screen instructions for loading your mat.

4 Once your faux leather is cut, gently weed away from your mat. You can either do this with your weeder, or just pulling with your hand.

5 Using your spatula to help, peel away your keyring shapes from the mat.

6 Load your iron-on on to your mat using your brayer. Make sure to load the iron-on shiny carrier sheet side down and that 'Mirror' is selected in Design Space for your font.

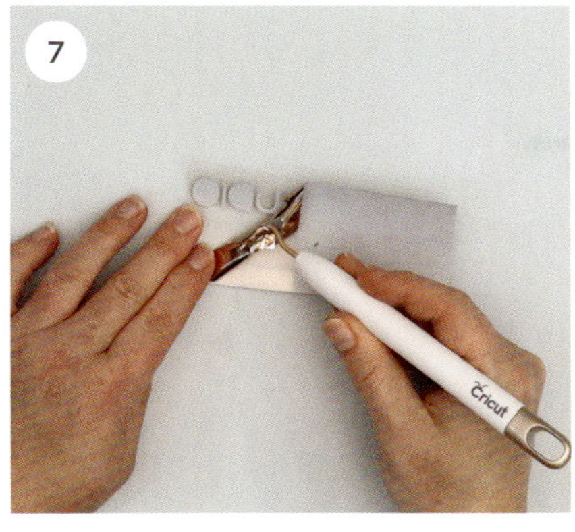

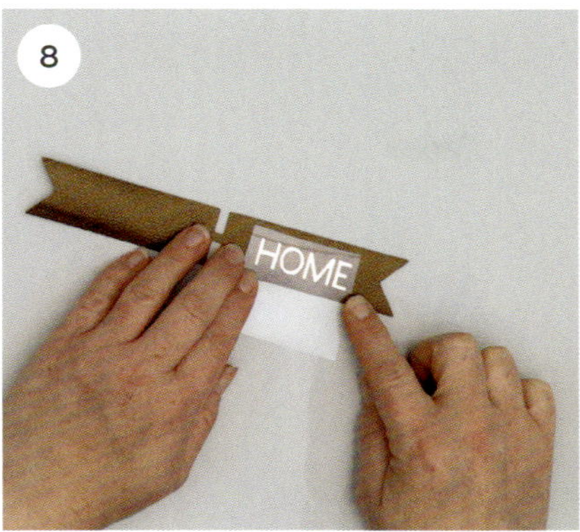

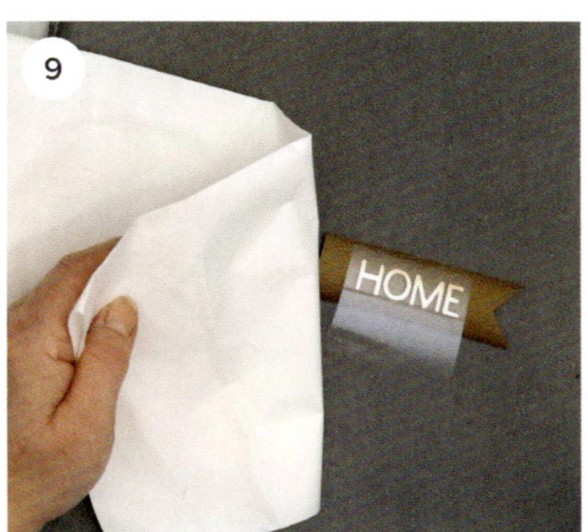

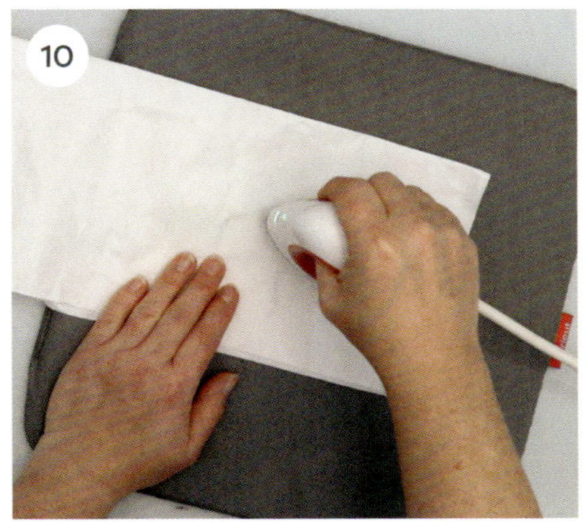

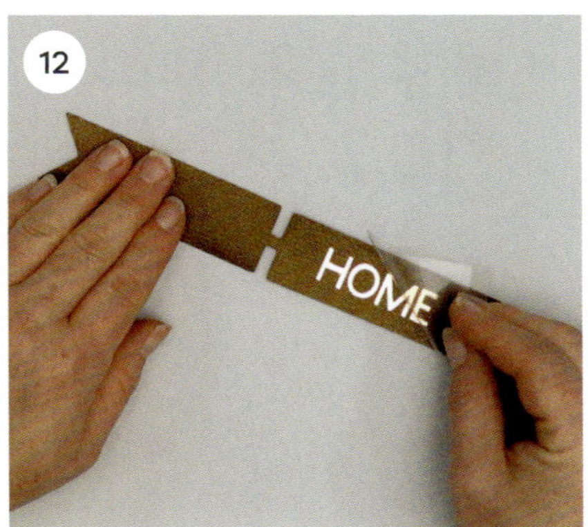

7 Once cut, weed out your designs.

8 Position your text in the middle of one side of your cut-out shape. Turn on your EasyPress Mini ready for heating as it will take a little while to warm up. Check the Cricut Heat Guide for latest advice on what temperature and time settings are recommended for your chosen materials and your EasyPress version.

9 To protect the faux leather in the heating process, place something like a sheet of Butcher Paper, baking paper or even a sheet of photocopy paper over the iron-on.

10 Use your EasyPress Mini to transfer the iron-on to your faux leather. Keep your EasyPress moving to make sure your faux leather does not get marked by the heat.

11 Once the heating is complete, leave the carrier sheet in position. Allow to cool. If you're making more than one keyring, repeat the steps with your second keyring.

12 Once cool, peel back the carrier sheet.

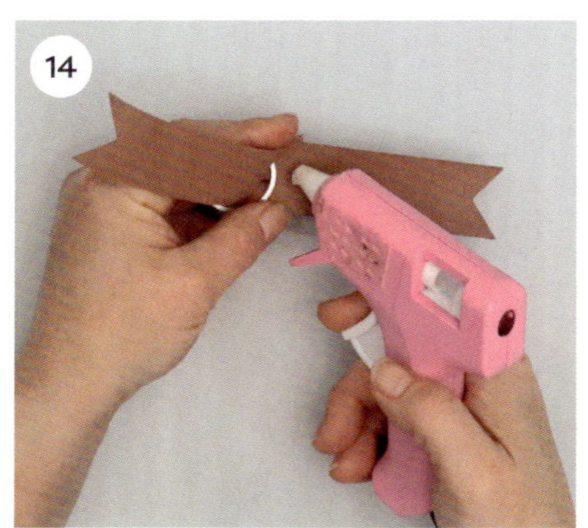

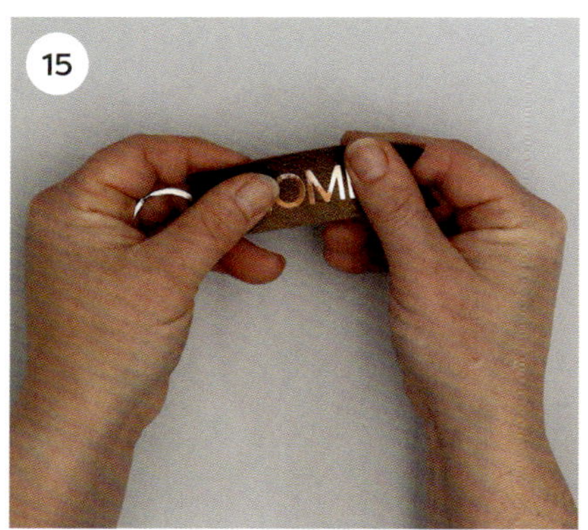

13 Slide your keyring loop on to your keyring shape until it gets to the middle notch point.

14 Using your hot glue gun, add glue on the back of your keyring...

15 ... before folding back and joining together, lining up the shapes.

16 And you are done! One personalized keyring.

GOING BEYOND THE MAKE

You can use faux leather for making some really cute fashion accessories such as bows or even jewellery.

It is also excellent for covering plain notebooks that you could then decorate using iron-on – great for making unique, personalized stationery!

Paper Leaf Wreath

I love wreaths! In fact, I don't just have one for Christmas, I actually have one hanging on our front door all year round. This paper one wouldn't withstand being outdoors, but it would look beautiful inside the home or used in celebrations. It would make a beautiful table centrepiece for use with (faux) candles, or simply on a shelf as a stylish decoration.

YOU WILL NEED

MACHINE
- [ ] Cricut Machine and Blade (I used Cricut Maker 3 and Fine Point Blade for Cricut Maker)

TOOLS
- [ ] Cricut LightGrip Mat
- [ ] Cricut Brayer
- [ ] Cricut Weeder
- [ ] Cricut Spatula
- [ ] Cricut Scoring Stylus
- [ ] Glue Gun
- [ ] Cricut Scissors (optional)
- [ ] Cricut Scraper (optional)

MATERIALS
- [ ] Green Cardstock
- [ ] Wreath Hoop
- [ ] White Felt Balls

IMAGES
- [ ] Design Space Leaves SVG #M505DCD8D

NOTES

- I am using my Leaves image in Design Space for this project, but you could use this technique with whatever leaf shape or image that you would like.

- You can use any card or paper you like, but the leaves do work better on a thicker, heavier weight gsm to ensure the leaves keep their shape and provide structure once scored and folded.

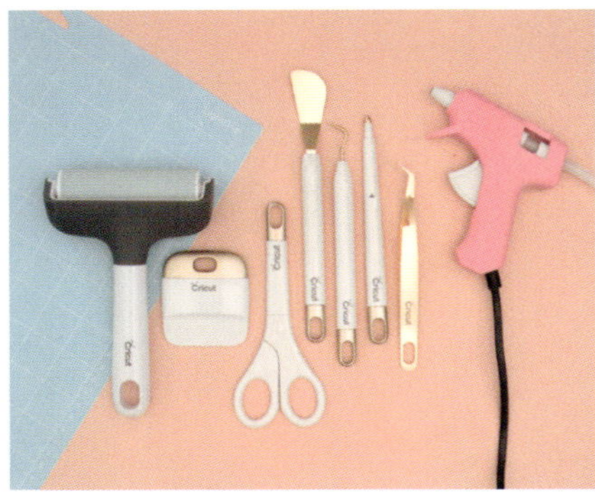

1 Access the Leaves SVG, or your chosen image, within Design Space. I have chosen the LightGrip Mat for use with this cardstock. Use your brayer to smooth out and make sure your paper or card is fully attached to the mat. The brayer is very useful when using an older mat that has started to lose its stick.

2 Duplicate the 'Leaf Trio' design as many times as you require in Design Space. I decided to cut each size individually so I could choose varying amounts of each. I chose to cut two different green colours of the largest leaf, two different green colours of the medium size and just one of the small.

Large leaf: 21 x 2 darker-tone greens (42 leaves in total)
Medium leaf: 15 x 2 mid-tone greens (30 in total)
Small leaf: 30 in just one fresh tone

How many leaves you need will depend on whether you change the Leaves size in Design Space and also how large or small your wreath hoop is. Follow the on-screen instructions for loading your papers and cutting. Make sure you select the correct material, such as 'Medium Cardstock', for example, when requested and your relevant mat size.

3 Once your machine has finished cutting, weed any excess paper away from your mat using your weeder and/or spatula. The spatula tool is very useful for gently peeling papers away from your mat.

REMINDER Either keep your paper scraps for smaller projects or pop into the recycling.

4 Gently peel each leaf away from the mat (your spatula can help with this). You can also bend the mat slightly, which helps the leaves naturally come away from your mat too.

5 Once you have peeled off all your leaves, put them all to one side, before moving on to the next colours. Repeat with your remaining paper or card colours until you have cut out all your leaves.

6 You may note that some of the shapes you have cut out leave marks on the mat – don't worry, the mat isn't damaged! You can just continue to use the mat as normal on top of these marks.

REMINDER Once you have cut out all of your leaves, remember to put the liner back to keep your mat clean.

7 Gather all your leaves together.

8 Take one of the leaves. With the scoring stylus, you could choose to add some 'Score Lines' to each leaf before cutting in Design Space. The machine would then do this step for you. However, I prefer to manually use the scoring stylus on this project so that each leaf isn't scored in exactly the same way as it makes them look slightly more natural. Score each leaf down the centre. Some I chose to do all the way down the leaf, others just halfway.

9 Gently fold the leaves along the fold line to create a natural crease in the leaf.

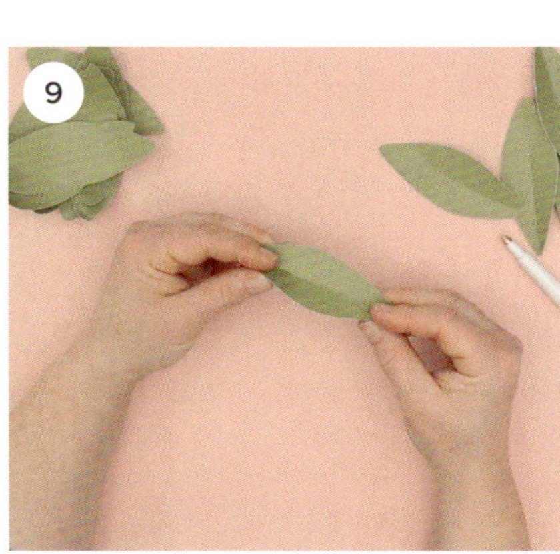

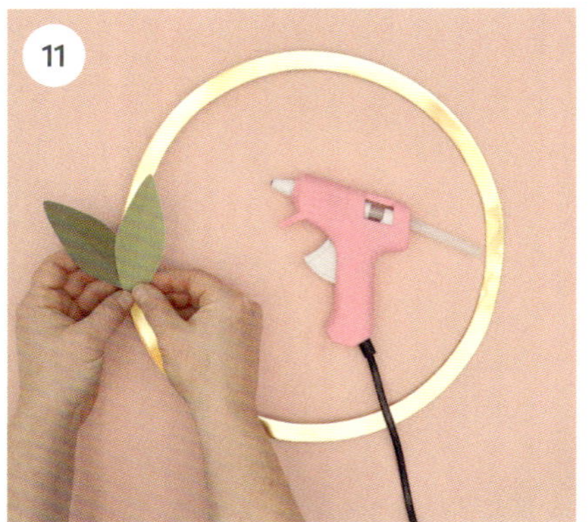

10 Repeat with the rest of the leaves. On some of the medium and small leaves, I have scored and bent down the back of the leaves to mix up the direction of the curve of each leaf.

11 You will now need your wreath hoop and hot glue gun. I chose this wreath hoop as it has a nice wide and flat base, which helps when attaching the leaves, but you could use any wreath hoop you like. Use small dots of glue to attach the leaves on to the hoop. Try to vary the colours and sizes as you go to allow for a tonal and natural effect.

12 Continue working your way around the wreath hoop, continuing to mix up the colours and sizes. If you get near the end and find you need more leaves, simply make some more so that the leaves go all the way around.

13 Once you get back to the first leaves, tuck in and glue the final ones underneath so it becomes a continuous loop.

14 Now you can start to add the felt berries. Using the hot glue again, secure randomly around the wreath wherever you think looks best. In some places, I have added two berries together. I have used 18 felt balls in total.

15 You are now finished! A lovely paper wreath.

GOING BEYOND THE MAKE

I have used soft olive tones of green card alongside the white berries, which I think makes it look very classical and an all-year-round decoration. You could make these leaves in bright green card and use red felt balls, which would make it feel much more 'festive'. You could also make the leaves multicoloured in all colours of the rainbow – they don't need to be just green.

This 'Leaf Trio' SVG is the same image used in the Infusible Ink Wreath Cushion project on page 122. It just goes to show you how flexible SVG files can be – used here in paper and in iron-on and Infusible Ink there.

Autumn Garland

I often make paper garlands for birthday parties or events, but I think they could actually make great seasonal home decorations. I have used a very autumnal colour palette, but you could create this in fresh greens or, in fact, in a whole rainbow of colours.

YOU WILL NEED

MACHINE

- Cricut Machine and Blade (I used Cricut Maker 3 and Cricut Fine Point Blade for Maker)

TOOLS

- Cricut StandardGrip Mat
- Cricut Brayer
- Cricut Weeder
- Cricut Spatula
- Glue Gun or Glue
- Cricut Scissors
- Cricut Scraper (optional)

MATERIALS

- Selection of paper and/or cardstock. I have chosen browns, oranges and greens for the leaves, and reds, white and grey for the toadstool
- Ribbon or Twine

IMAGES

- Exclusive Oak Leaf SVG
- Exclusive Toadstool SVG

NOTE

- Be sure not to hang the paper garland above a fireplace with an open flame!
- I have chosen to use a hot glue gun as I find it quick drying and secure. Other glues may work, but be sure to test them on a small piece of scrap card before proceeding with the main project.
- You can use any card or paper you like, but both the toadstools and the oak leaves do work better on a thicker, heavier weight gsm to ensure the smaller delicate cuts do not tear.

1 Upload the exclusive Oak Leaf and Toadstool SVG files to your Canvas in Design Space and duplicate as many times as you require. I cut 48 toadstools in total. I used 3 shades of red card, cutting 12 at a time in the uploaded SVG size, and another 12 slightly smaller using a brighter shade of red. Both the leaf and the toadstool have small gaps at the top to allow you to thread your ribbon or twine through. Make sure this gap stays large enough for whatever you are using to hang them. I also cut varying amounts of the different-coloured oak leaves depending on the cardstock I had in the autumnal colours. Adjust for however long you want your garland and how condensed you would like the leaves to be. I have created one garland with just leaves, one garland with just toadstools and one that is a mixture of both.

2 Follow the on-screen instructions for loading your papers and cutting. Make sure you select the correct material, such as 'Medium Cardstock' for example, when requested and your relevant mat size.

3 Once your machine has finished cutting, weed any excess paper away from your mat using your weeder.

4 Gently peel each toadstool away from the mat. The smaller spots on the toadstool should hopefully remain on your mat (doing some of the weeding job for you).

5 I find it easiest to use your spatula for gently peeling the cardstock away from the mat.

6 Once you have removed all of your main cardstock cut-outs, use your scraper to collect up all the smaller remaining pieces left on your mat.

7 Repeat steps 2 to 6 for your leaves.

8 Once all of your leaves and toadstool shapes are cut out, you are ready to add to your ribbon to construct the garland(s). Thread your ribbon through the small gap at the top of each leaf. Keep them approximately the same distance apart.

9 The toadstools consist of three pieces that will need to be glued together. I found this is easiest to do once attached on to the garland. If you do it beforehand, it makes them difficult to thread on. Thread the cream toadstool base with the gap at the top on to the ribbon.

10 Using your glue gun or glue, attach the red piece into position. Be careful to not add glue at the very top where the ribbon or twine goes. This will allow your toadstool to still move. Next, add your grey stalk on to the cream base.

11 Continue adding on leaves, mixing them up to include both these and toadstools.

12 And you are done! I think these are lovely when combined with different garlands hung together, one mixed, alongside one just leaves and one just toadstools.

GOING BEYOND THE MAKE

These oak leaves and toadstool SVG images would also look lovely cut out in felt as little individual hanging decorations. The oak leaf would also look particularly lovely in the Cricut soft leather – you could get creative with jewellery design, a bag tag or even a keyring!

Botanical Towel

Reminiscent of block printing, this simple botanical shape in vivid blue makes for a simple but stunning Infusible Ink project. This soft microfibre towel could be used in the bathroom or kitchen or even on holiday! Cricut advises that you should craft with Infusible Ink in a well-ventilated room.

YOU WILL NEED

MACHINES

- Cricut Machine and Blade (I used Cricut Explore 3 and Fine Point Blade for Cricut Explore)
- Cricut EasyPress Mini

TOOLS

- Cricut LightGrip Mat
- Cricut Brayer
- Cricut Scraper
- Cricut Spatula
- Cricut Scissors
- Cricut Tweezers

MATERIALS

- 100% Polyester Microfibre Towel
- Cricut Infusible Ink Transfer Sheets (I have used True Blue)
- Cricut Infusible Ink Butcher Paper

IMAGES

- Exclusive Botanical Leaf SVG

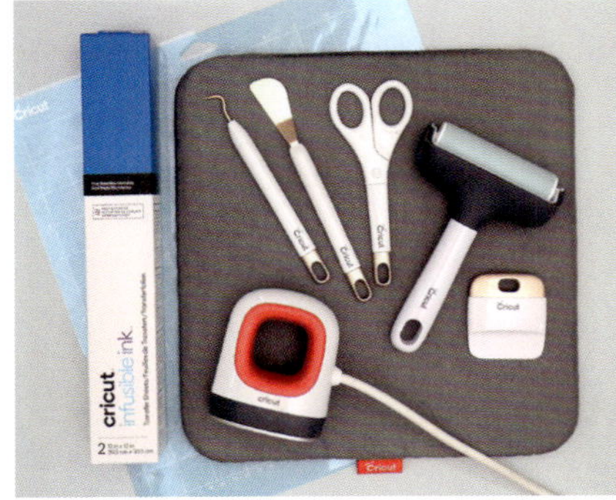

NOTES

- I recommend checking the Cricut Heat Guide for the latest advice on what temperature and time settings are recommended for your chosen materials and your EasyPress version. For this project, I've used a 100% polyester microfibre towel, which is not an official Cricut blank, so you will have to use the Heat Guide as a generic guide. I selected 'any polyester blank' instead to let me know what temperature to use.

- I have used a LightGrip Mat here as it is a brand new mat and very sticky, but I would usually use a StandardGrip Mat for Infusible Ink transfer sheets. Make sure you use your brayer tool and that everything is securely stuck down.

- Normally, I recommend using an EasyPress that is larger than your cut out Infusible Ink to ensure even and smooth transfer of your design. However, this microfibre towel creases very easily, so using the EasyPress Mini gives you greater flexibility to make sure everything is nice and smooth.

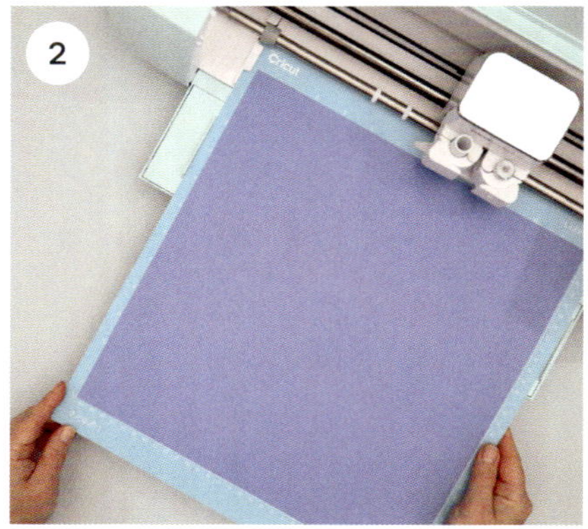

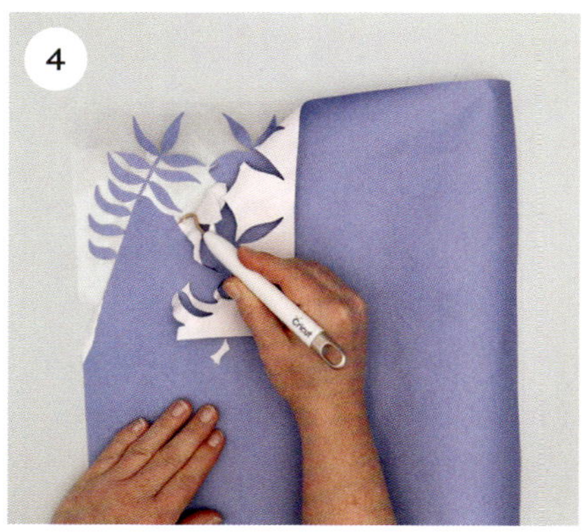

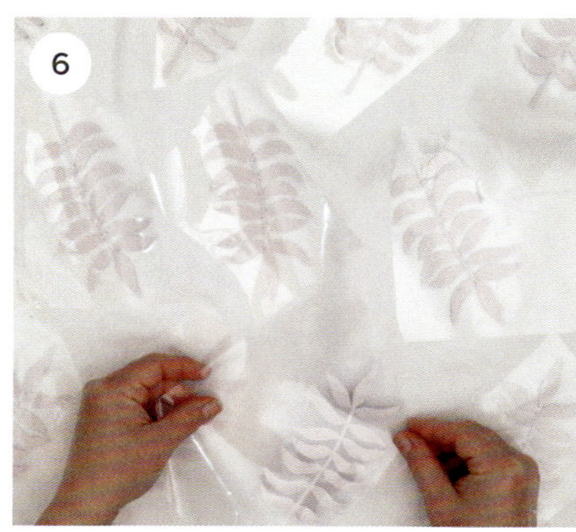

1 Select your mat and add your Infusible Ink Transfer Sheet. Make sure you have the shiny carrier sheet face-down and matte transfer sheet face-up. Use your brayer to make sure everything is smooth and air-bubble free.

2 Upload your Botanical Leaves SVG file and add to your Design Space Canvas. I have duplicated the leaf shape several times so I have plenty to fully go across my towel. You'll need to adapt this according to your own towel blank size. Follow the on-screen instructions for cutting the design and loading the mat and materials when requested. I used four sheets of Infusible Ink for this towel size.

3 Once your design has been cut, peel it away gently from your mat.

4 Using your weeder, weed your design. When you weed any Infusible Ink layers, the thick paper-style transfer sheet sort of 'cracks' off the carrier sheet. Pull it up gently and carefully so that the paper does not tear. If you do end up with small pieces of paper you can leave these in place as long as they do not contain any trace of the Infusible Ink, as this will transfer under heat.

5 Using your scissors, cut out each leaf so they are ready to apply to your towel. Make sure there is plenty of carrier sheet around each leaf, so there will be some support around your design when sticking into position on your towel.

6 Unfold your towel and lay out your leaf designs, colour-side face down. It might take several attempts until you are happy with where everything sits, but just peel each one up and move it. The colour won't go on to your towel until you add your heat.

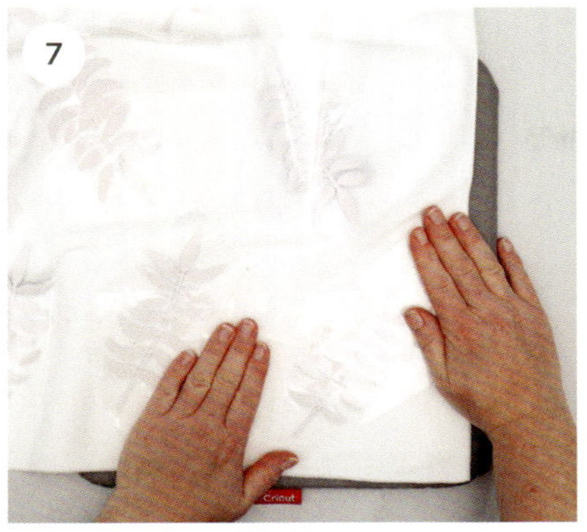

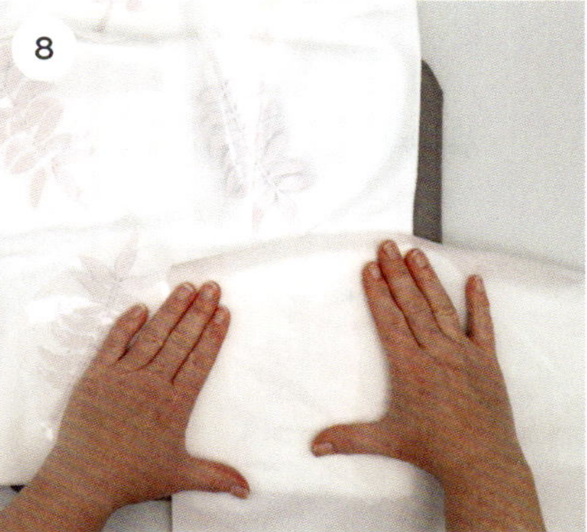

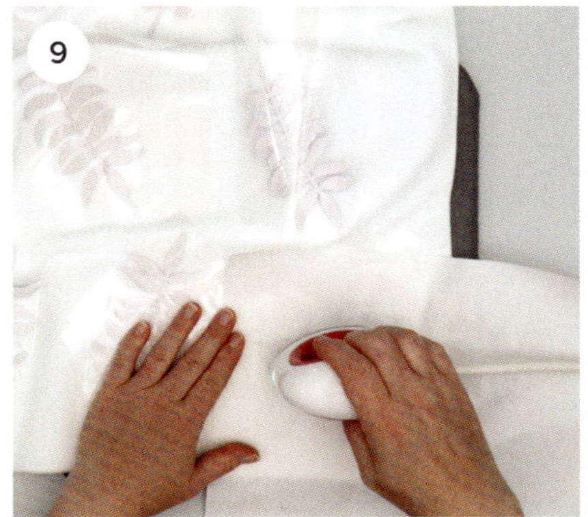

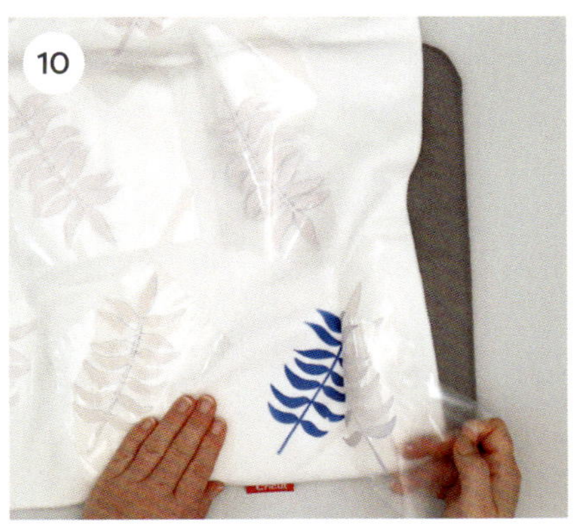

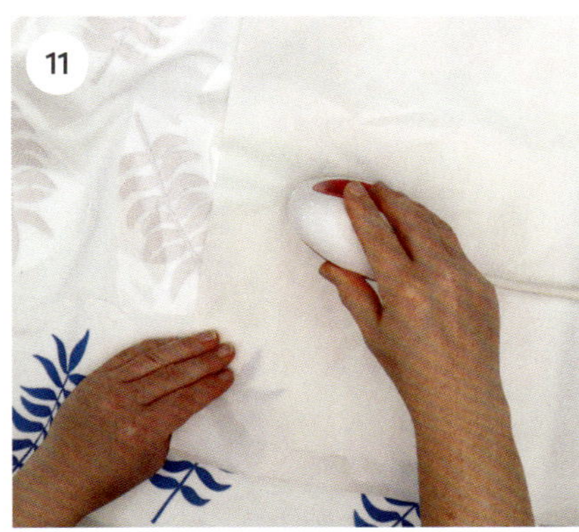

7 Make sure your towel is positioned on your EasyPress Mat and smooth everything out with your hands.

8 Add a piece of Butcher Paper where your leaf is ready to be heated.

9 Using your EasyPress Mini start to heat your leaf design. It is important to keep it moving, as too much heat in one area could damage your polyester towel. Don't push too firmly as you move as this may also move your Infusible Ink, which will end up creating a 'ghosting' effect (where the design is heated in different positions and you can see the shape multiple times). Just use a gentle but continuous pressure. Allow to cool and move on to the next leaf, heating in the same way.

10 Once your first leaf is fully cool, peel away to reveal your design.

11 Work across the towel, heating each leaf in the same way. Repeat steps 7–10 with all of your other leaves.

12 And you are done! A vivid and fresh botanical towel.

GOING BEYOND THE MAKE

Why not experiment with using multiple colours for this design? You could even cross the leaves over one another for a layered effect. This leaf shape would also look fabulous cut out in iron-on and used in the Fiesta Table Mat project on page 135, or cut out in vinyl and added to a water bottle as on page 130.

Ceramic Coasters

If you own an EasyPress, creating coasters is one of the simplest Infusible Ink projects you could ever make. The round ceramic Cricut blanks are heavy, glossy and great quality. You could adhere vinyl on to these if you wanted to, but they truly come to life when combined with Infusible Ink, using either transfer sheets or pens. Once your design is heat-transferred, the depth of colour these coasters provide is just so vibrant and beautiful. They are perfect for your dining-room or coffee table.

YOU WILL NEED

MACHINE

- Cricut EasyPress

TOOLS

- Cricut EasyPress Mat
- Cricut Scissors
- Cricut Spatula (optional)

MATERIALS

- Cricut Ceramic Coaster Blanks
- Cricut Infusible Ink Transfer Sheet (I have used Blue Paint Splash)
- Cricut Infusible Ink Butcher Paper
- Cricut Heat-Resistant Tape

NOTES

- There are also Cricut square coasters with a cork back.
- It is very tempting to just use standard sticky tape instead of heat-resistant tape to secure your design into position but I would highly recommend that you don't! It melts under the high temperatures of your EasyPress, can be a fire risk and creates quite a sticky mess on your blank. (I learnt this the hard way!)
- Please keep your EasyPress on the recommended storage plate when switched on as it can get extremely hot. Use your EasyPress on a flat surface.

1 When you take your Infusible Ink sheet out of the box, it will be concealed in a black pouch that helps protect the ink surface from light damage. Remove this from the box.

2 Cut open the black pouch and remove your transfer sheets from inside. Save this black pouch in case you have any remaining Infusible Ink you want to store for future projects. To see more on storage of Infusible Ink, see the 'Materials' section on page 27 at the beginning of the book.

3 Trim your Infusible Ink sheet, making sure it is bigger than your coaster size. You may prefer to place your coaster blank on to the sheet and draw around it as a template before cutting out. I have chosen to cut it into a square and wrap the sheet around to the reverse of the coaster.

4 There is a shiny side and a matte side to your coaster. The shiny side is the top of your coaster. Place the shiny side down on to the transfer sheet design. Using your heat-resistant tape, fix into position. Note that when you heat it, the design will also transfer here on to the matte back of the coaster. To follow the 'splash pad' design I wanted to wrap the sheet around to show some of the colour on the sides of the coaster.

5 You are now ready to transfer the design on to the coasters using your EasyPress. Turn on your EasyPress to give it time to heat up. Place your EasyPress mat on a smooth, flat surface.

6 Next place several layers of Infusible Ink Butcher Paper on to your EasyPress mat. These layers will protect the mat from picking up the colour of your designs and being marked.

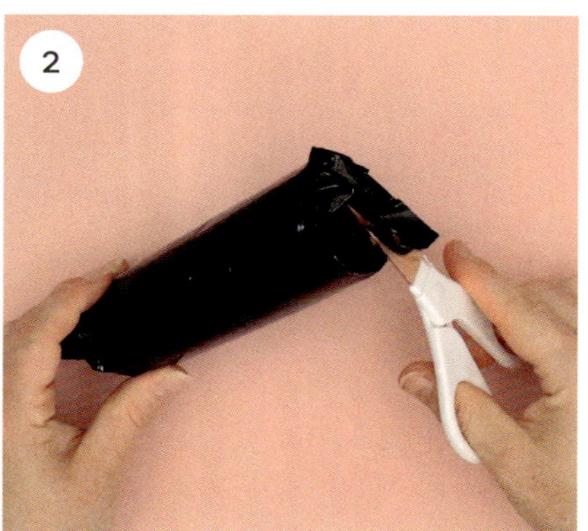

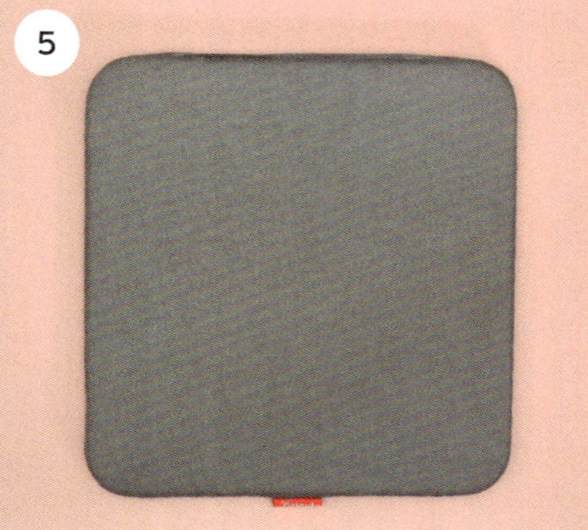

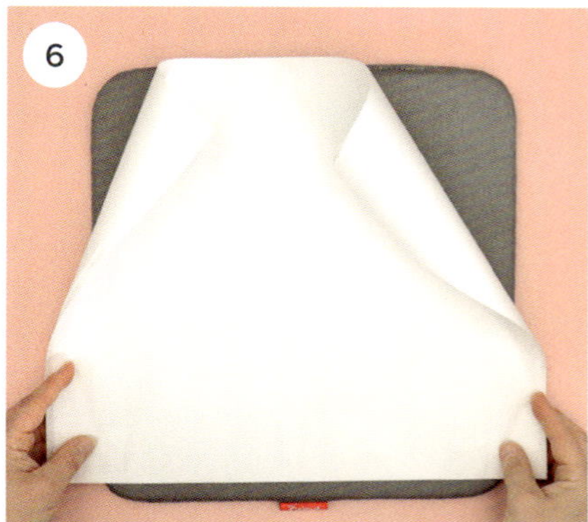

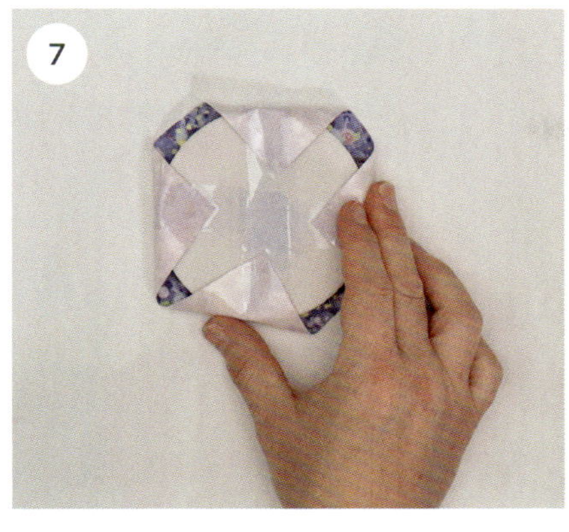

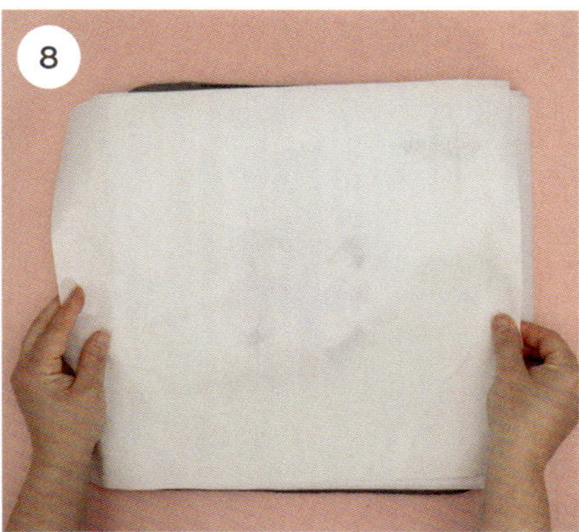

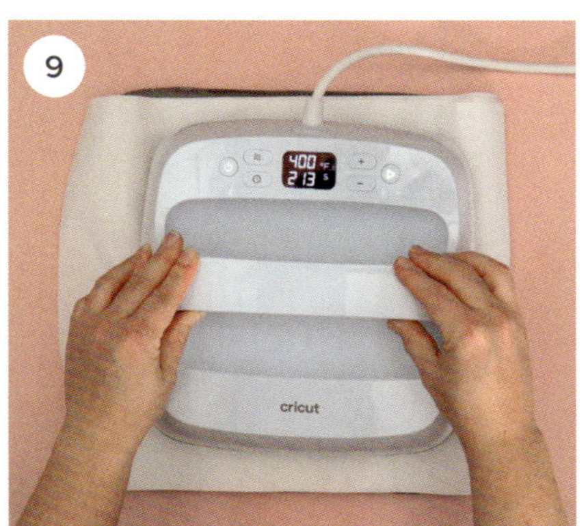

7 Place your coaster on to the Butcher Paper. You need the Infusible Ink design face-up, and the coaster shiny side face-down.

8 Place an additional sheet or 2 of the Butcher Paper on top of your coaster.

9 Check the Cricut Heat Guide for the latest instructions of temperatures and timings suitable for your EasyPress model. Try not to move your EasyPress in the heating process so that the design doesn't move.

10 Once heated, allow everything to completely cool. The ceramic will be extremely hot, so this is very important for safety and to allow the design to 100% transfer correctly. You will see here in this image that some of the design has come through on to the Butcher Paper.

11 Once cool, peel back the top layer of Butcher Paper.

12 Peel back your heat-resistant tape.

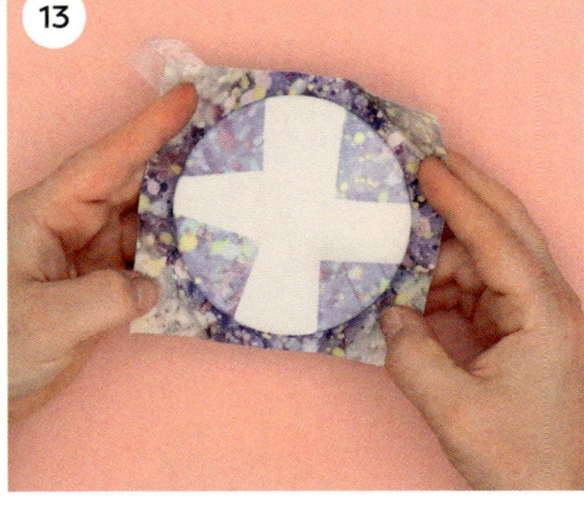

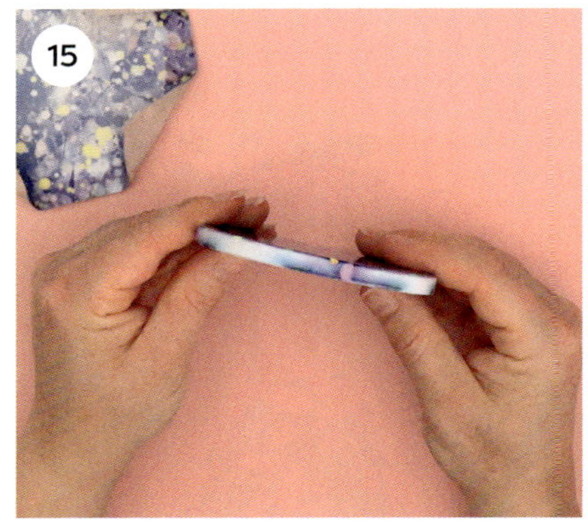

13 Open out the transfer sheet. You can see here where some of the design has transferred on to the back of the coaster wherever the Infusible Ink has come into contact with the blank.

14 Remove the transfer sheet and reveal your design... Just look at how vibrant the colours are!

15 You can see here how the sides of the coaster have additionally picked up the colour, which is ideal for this paint-splash look, but you may want to cut out a circle just for the top, as I mentioned.

GOING BEYOND THE MAKE

This project uses an existing Infusible Ink Transfer Sheet, but you could cut out a shape or design from the sheet using your machine to then transfer on to the coaster. The citrus fruit images in the table runner and napkins project on page 70 would really suit the round shape here. Or you could get creative, doodling using the Infusible Ink pens. You could also transfer your Infusible Ink drawings on to the other Cricut compatible blanks.

MORE IDEAS

1 You can also simply use photocopy paper and Infusible Ink pens to draw your own designs before heating in the same way as a transfer sheet. You could use your machine to draw out an image, or you could get creative, sketching whatever you like before heating in the same way. Here I have taken a selection of the green pens and drawn a repeating leaf pattern.

2 I used the heat-resistant tape to fix into position, then heated in the same way as the transfer sheet.

3 It's such a simple and fun crafty idea to turn your drawings and doodles into a beautiful home-made product.

4 This is a particularly great idea to do with kids. This is a coaster design my eldest child drew when he was very young – one of the first times he drew his family. This would make such a great Mother's or Father's Day gift. Just let them get creative drawing and colouring whatever they like in these special pens, before transferring the Infusible Ink.

REMEMBER Any Infusible Ink designs transfer in reverse, so consider this with any text as it could end up being backwards.

Daisy Apron

I love flowers and nature and I am really drawn to creating with them. This simple daisy design, scattered across the deep navy blue, really lifts what would be just a plain cotton apron. Cricut iron-on is perfect for personalizing all sorts of clothing, and creating a unique apron for your home is no exception.

YOU WILL NEED

MACHINES

- Cricut Machine and Blade (I used Cricut Maker 3 and Fine Point Blade for Cricut Maker)
- Cricut EasyPress Mini

TOOLS

- Cricut StandardGrip Mat
- Cricut Weeder
- Cricut Scissors
- Cricut Brayer
- Cricut Spatula (optional)
- Cricut Tweezers (optional)
- Cricut Scraper (optional)
- Cricut EasyPress Mat

MATERIALS

- Cricut Everyday Iron-On in your choice of colours (I have used white and yellow)
- 100% Cotton Apron

IMAGES

- Design Space Daisy SVG #M432FCB49

NOTES

- I have chosen a 100% cotton crossbody-style apron. You could, of course, do this with any style of fabric apron.
- I am using my Daisy image in Design Space for this project, but you could use this technique with whatever image you like.
- For most iron-on designs you need to make sure you use the 'Mirror' function in Design Space, but as these look almost the same both ways around, this does not need to be activated.

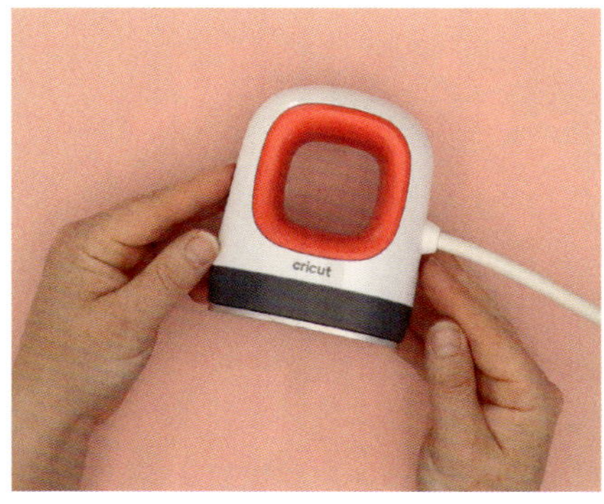

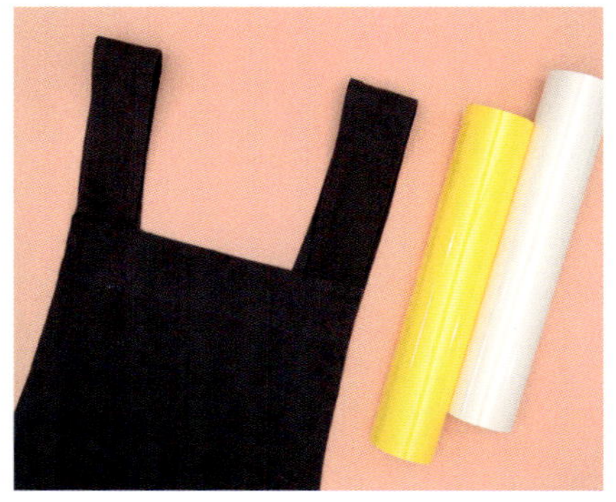

1 Access the daisy or your choser image in Design Space. Attach your iron-on to your mat with the shiny carrier-sheet face-down (you want the matte iron-on to face upwards). Alternatively, you can load your Smart Materials directly into your machine. Follow the on-screen instructions for cutting all of your colours out. I have duplicated the daisy in Design Space to cut 32 in total. I also adjusted the daisy size to be 3in (7.6cm).

2 Use the brayer to ensure everything is smooth and free of air bubbles.

3 Trim out your cut-out designs, reserving any spare iron-on for future projects.

4 Using your weeder, weed out your designs.

5 Once your designs are fully weeded, cut out each element of your design, ready for attaching on to your apron.

6 Turn on your EasyPress ready for making as it will need a small amount of time to heat up. Check the Cricut Heat Guide for latest advice on what temperature and time settings are recommended for your chosen materials and your EasyPress version. Following the Heat Guide recommendations, pre-heat where you want to attach a daisy to your apron.

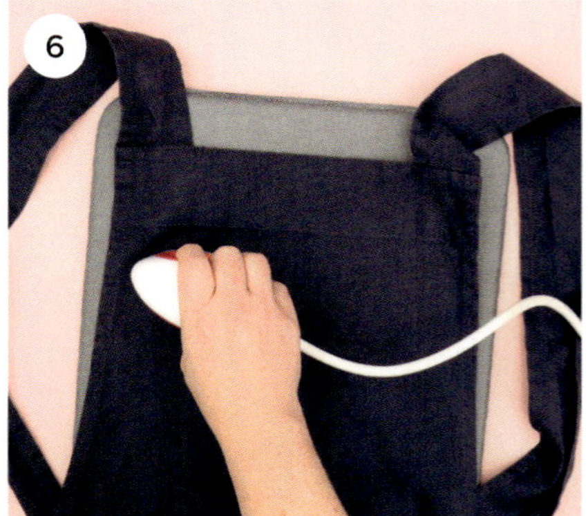

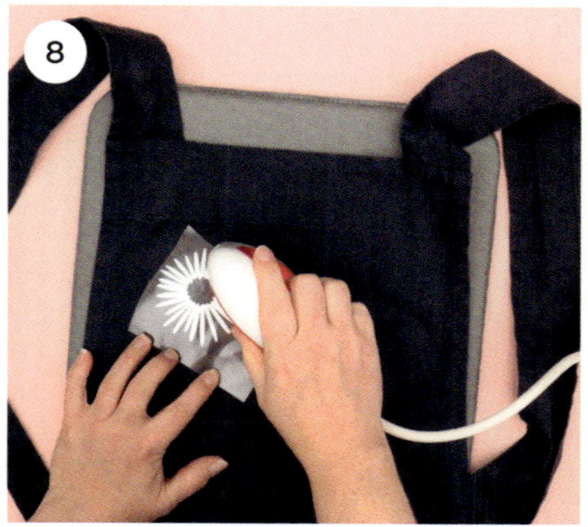

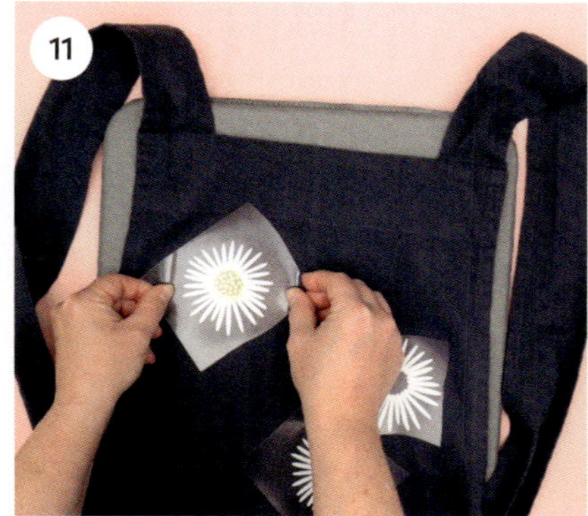

7 Lay the petal part of the design where you would like it to be positioned. Be careful as the apron will be hot from the pre-heating.

8 Following the Heat Guide, use your EasyPress to attach the iron-on to your apron.

9 Continue attaching your daisy petals. You can either scatter them randomly across your apron or keep them neatly together in a more uniform pattern. Once everything is cool, peel back your carrier sheet carefully to see if anything hasn't adhered. You can always re-cover with any carrier sheets and repeat the heating again.

10 Now place the centre part of the daisy into position.

11 Make sure to cover the entire daisy with a piece of carrier sheet.

12 Heat again to adhere the centre part of the design.

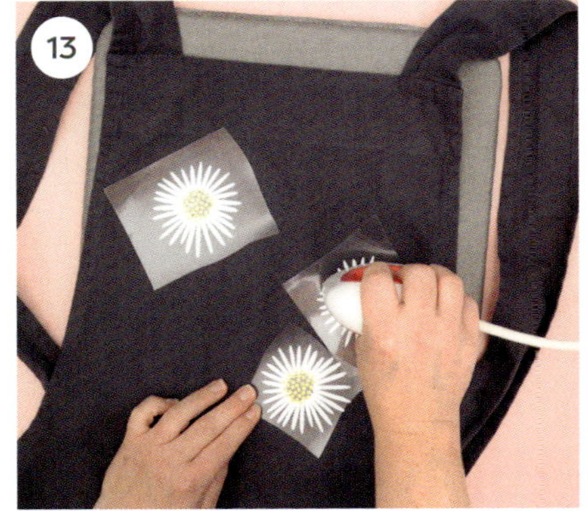

13 Repeat with your other daisy centres.

14 Peel back the carrier-sheet pieces checking to make sure everything is attached securely.

15 Repeat across all of the apron.

16 And you are finished! One lovely, daisy-filled apron.

GOING BEYOND THE MAKE

You could make personalized aprons in this same way for children, at school or for crafting. The Daisy image has also been used in the Lunchbox project on page 130. The daisies would also look lovely on the Tea Towel idea on page 64, or even converted into Infusible Ink for the Ceramic Coasters on page 102.

Anemone Cosmetics Bag

This is a great project for combining Infusible Ink and Everyday and Glitter Iron-On to create a beautiful and personalized make. As well as the anemone on the front, I have chosen to put a monogram letter on the reverse side of the bag (page 119).

YOU WILL NEED

MACHINES

- Cricut Machine and Blade (I used Cricut Explore 3 and Fine Point Blade for Cricut Explore)
- Cricut EasyPress

TOOLS

- Cricut Mat (if required)
- Cricut Weeder
- Cricut Brayer
- Cricut Scraper
- Cricut Spatula
- Cricut Scissors

MATERIALS

- Cosmetic Bag Cricut Blank
- Cricut Infusible Ink Transfer Sheet (Splash Pad, Pink/Red)
- Cricut Infusible Ink Transfer Sheet (Watercolour, Green)
- Infusible Ink Butcher Paper
- Cricut Everyday Iron-On (Blush and Black)
- Cricut Glitter Iron-On (Mint and Rose Gold)

IMAGES

- Exclusive Anemone SVG

FONT

- A Child's Year

NOTES

- Use the colours in this order:
  Base layer of anemone (Infusible Ink, Splash Pad)
  Base Layer of leaf (Infusible Ink, Watercolour)
  Centre of anemone (iron-on, Black)
  Detail layer of anemone (iron-on, Blush)
  Detail layer of leaves (Glitter Iron-on, Mint)
  Font border (Iron-on, Blush)
  Font central main letter (Glitter Iron-on, Rose Gold)

- I chose to use the 'Offset' function in Design Space which allows me to add a thin border around my monogram letter.

- As you are using iron-on and Infusible Ink designs, please ensure to select the 'Mirror' function.

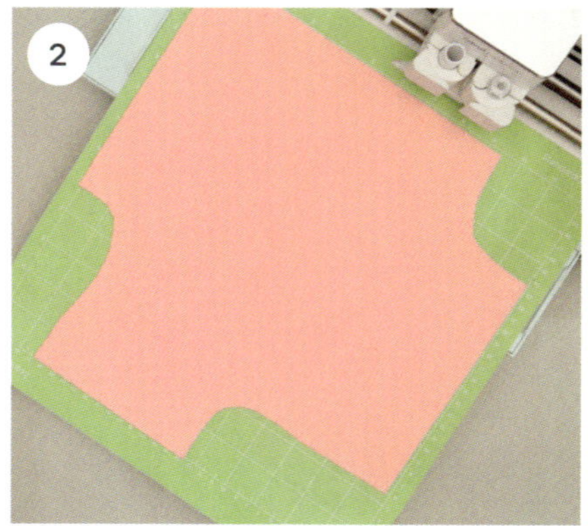

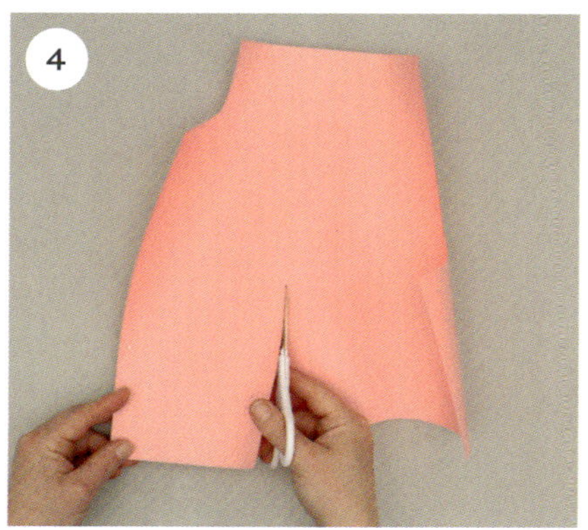

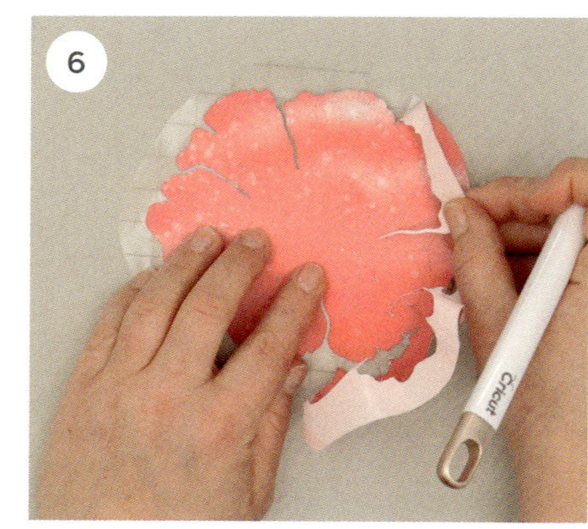

1 Open Design Space and upload the exclusive Anemone SVG file. Add the relevant materials on to your mat and use your brayer to ensure they are air-bubble and crease free. Alternatively load your Smart Materials directly into the machine. Make sure your materials are sized correctly for the machine you are using. I have deliberately chosen to use a large scrap to ensure that there isn't much waste.

2 Follow the on-screen instructions for cutting your anemone and font design, loading the relevant materials when requested. Ensure to load with the shiny, carrier sheet face-down.

3 When loading the Glitter Iron-On, load with the shiny, carrier sheet face-down – it often feels like you should have the glittery side upwards.

4 Using your scissors, trim back your design and put any spare aside for future projects.

5 Using your weeder, weed each layer of your design. On the black Everyday Iron-On for the centre of the anemone, weed back gently and slowly to ensure some of the smaller and more fiddlier parts do not tear or pull up.

6 When you weed the Infusible Ink layers, the thick transfer sheet sort of 'cracks' off the carrier sheet. Ensure to pull up gently and carefully so that the paper does not tear.

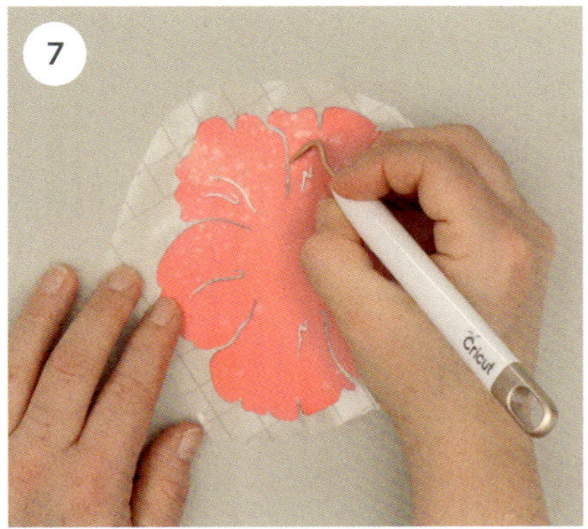

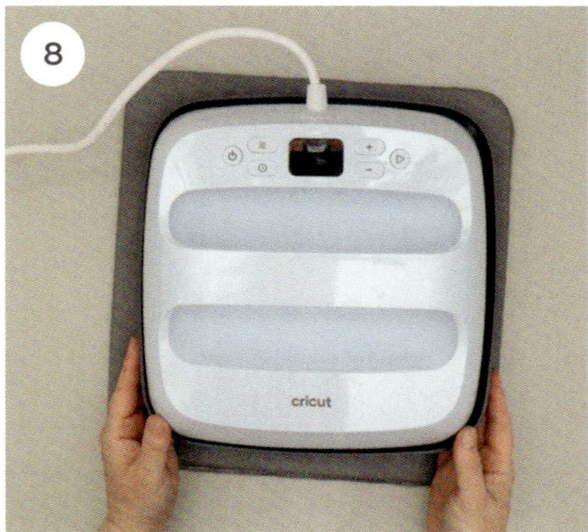

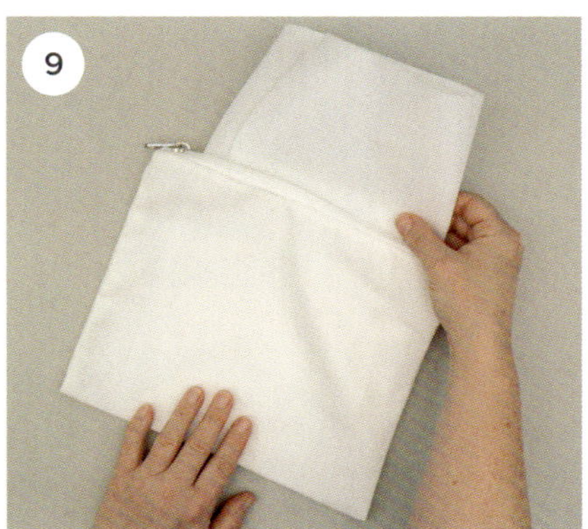

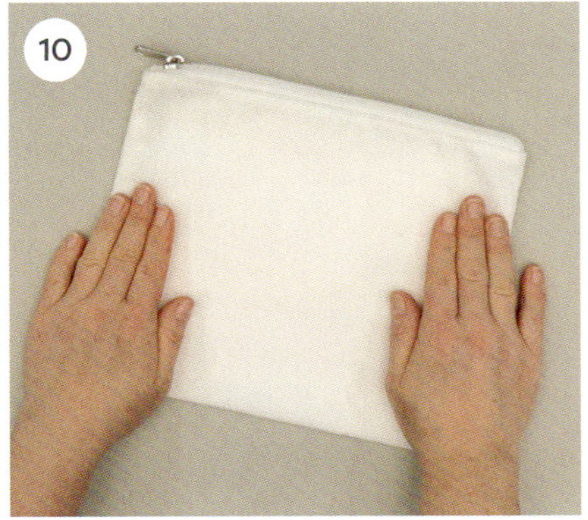

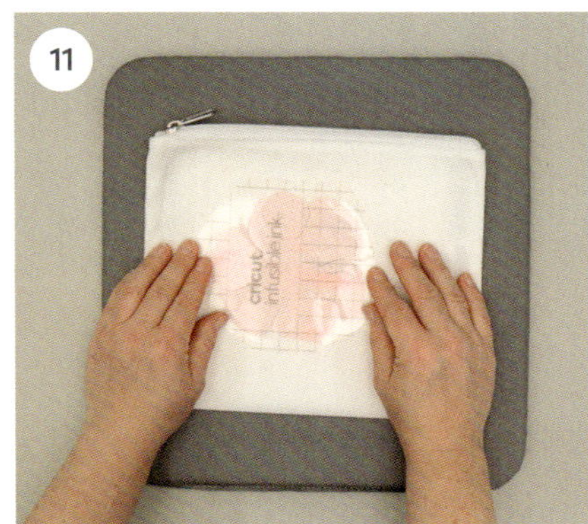

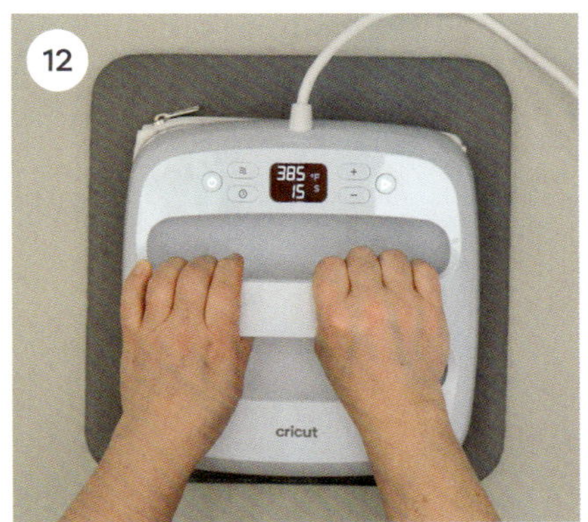

7 On some of the more fiddly parts, you may need to use your weeder to really scrape any smaller torn parts of the transfer sheet where required.

8 Turn on your EasyPress ready for making; this will give it time to heat up before transferring your designs.

9 Take your cosmetic bag blank and a sheet of Butcher Paper. Fold the paper up and place inside. This limits the possibility of your Infusible Ink transferring through to the other side of the bag under heat application.

10 Smooth down to ensure there are no creases.

11 Check the Cricut Heat Guide for the latest instructions of how to transfer your chosen materials. Place the first layer of your design on to your cosmetics bag. In this case, it is the Infusible Ink base layer of your anemone. The sticky carrier sheet should help to position this where you want.

12 Place another piece of Butcher Paper before following the instructions for applications. Be careful to make sure the EasyPress is nice and flat – and do not have the zip of your bag under the hot plate.

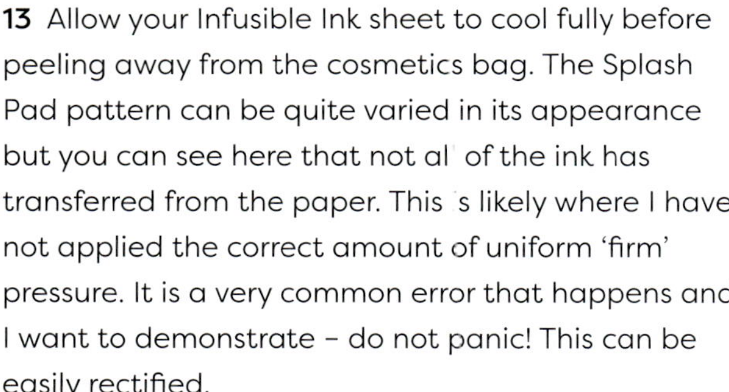

13 Allow your Infusible Ink sheet to cool fully before peeling away from the cosmetics bag. The Splash Pad pattern can be quite varied in its appearance but you can see here that not all of the ink has transferred from the paper. This is likely where I have not applied the correct amount of uniform 'firm' pressure. It is a very common error that happens and I want to demonstrate – do not panic! This can be easily rectified.

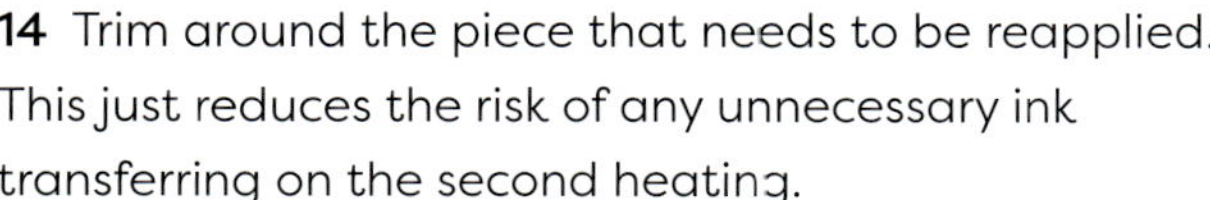

14 Trim around the piece that needs to be reapplied. This just reduces the risk of any unnecessary ink transferring on the second heating.

15 Line the piece up again to where it needs to go and, using your EasyPress again, follow the same heat and timings as the first time.

16 Allow to cool, before peeling away. You will see this time the complete design has now transferred without any gaps or problems in the design.

17 Place your Infusible Ink leaf piece into position. Re-add the carrier liner on to your main flower base so that you protect this when heating.

18 Add your Butcher Paper on top before heating in the same way following the heat guide instructions as your anemone flower base.

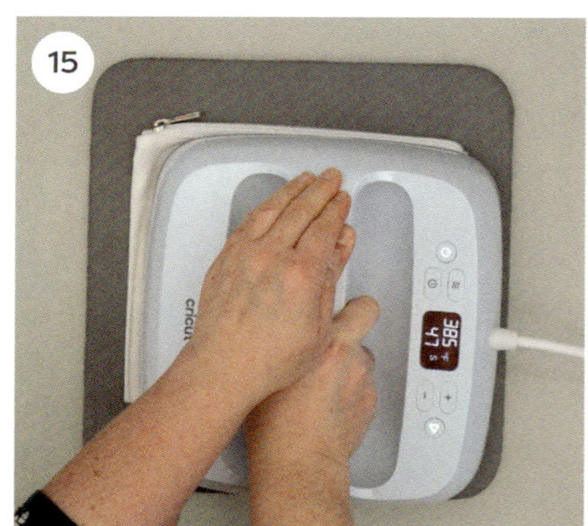

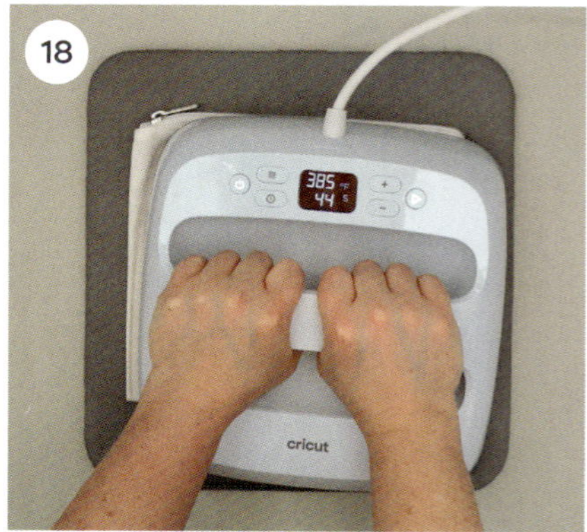

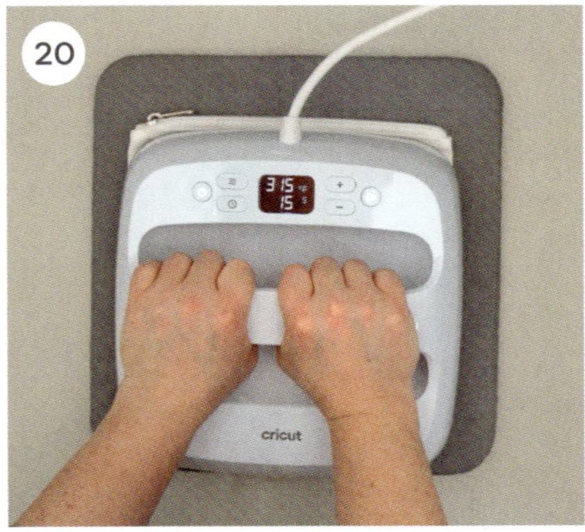

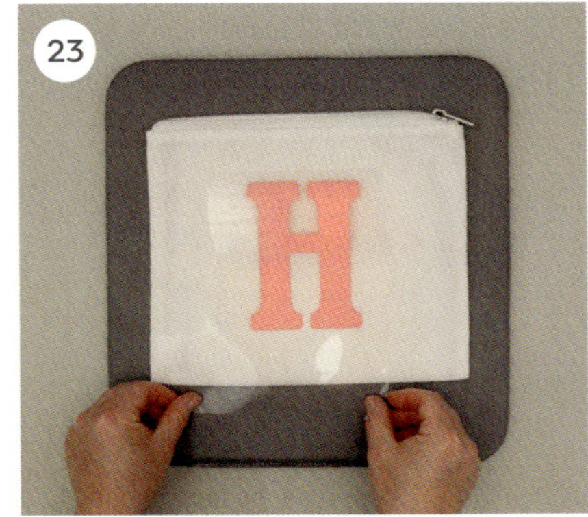

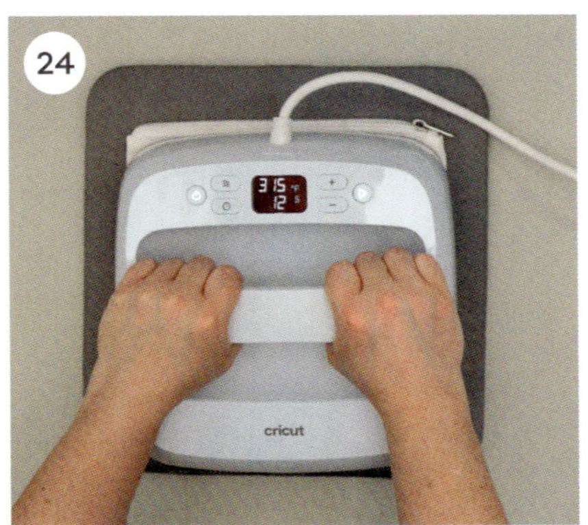

19 Allow everything to cool, before adding on your blush iron-on anemone detail layer.

20 Make sure your leaf and anemone base are completely covered in a protective, carrier-sheet layer before following the heat guide instructions for iron-on.

NOTE This will likely be different to the Infusible Ink so you may need to allow your EasyPress time to cool to the appropriate temperature.

21 Next, add your black anemone centre before heating in the say way as the anemone detail iron-on.

22 Finally, add the Glitter Iron-On detail to the leaves.

23 Turn your cosmetics bag over and add the first layer of your iron-on letter into position.

24 Use your EasyPress to fix into position, again following the heat guide instructions for your chosen material.

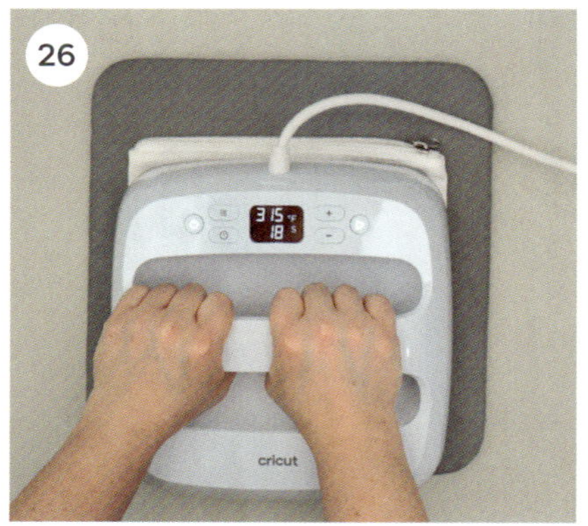

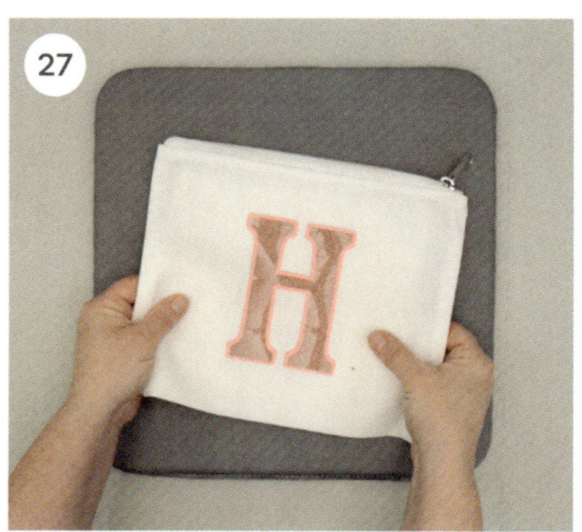

25 Allow everything to cool before finally, placing your Glitter Iron-On letter into position.

26 Heat again, following the Glitter Iron-On heat guide.

27 Allow to cool down.

28 Once cool, take the Butcher Paper out from inside of the bag.

29 And you are done! A beautifully personalized cosmetics bag.

GOING BEYOND THE MAKE

This project would make a lovely storage bag for the Reusable Face Wipes project on page 154 – they would make a lovely gift combined together.

This anemone design would look lovely on a table runner such as the one on page 70 or perhaps in vinyl on a water bottle. There is a more complex and festive 'layering' Infusible Ink and vinyl project in the Wreath Cushion on page 122 if you wanted to give this technique a try.

Wreath Cushion

I love Christmas! All the traditions and, of course, the decorations that come along with it. This wreath cushion adds a lovely festive touch, and is a great project for getting to grips with using multiple Cricut materials together.

YOU WILL NEED

MACHINES

- Cricut Machine and Blade (I used Cricut Joy and Fine Point Blade for Cricut Joy)
- Cricut EasyPress Mini

TOOLS

- Cricut LightGrip Mat (if not using Smart Materials)
- Cricut Brayer
- Cricut Scraper
- Cricut Spatula
- Cricut Scissors
- Cricut Tweezers (optional)
- Pencil (optional)

MATERIALS

- Cricut Pillow (Cushion) Blank
- Cricut Infusible Ink Transfer Sheets (Cherry Red, Watercolour Green and Bright Green)
- Infusible Ink Butcher Paper
- Cricut Everyday Iron-On (Kelly Green and Grass Green)
- Cricut Metallic Iron-On (Rose Gold and Red)
- Cricut Glitter Iron-On (Mint, Kelly Green and Red)

IMAGES

- Design Space Leaves SVG #M505DCD8D
- Design Space Berries SVG #M505DCD92

NOTES

- Please keep your EasyPress on the recommended storage plate when switched on. It can get very hot! Use your EasyPress to create this project on a flat surface.
- Whilst I am using my 'Leaves' and 'Berries' images in Design Space, you could use this technique with whatever images you like.

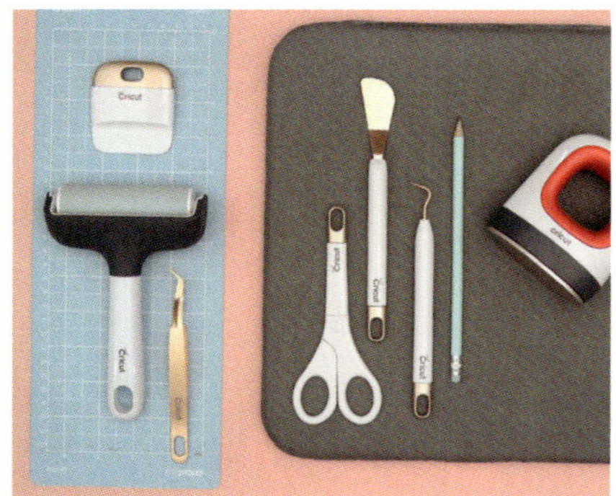

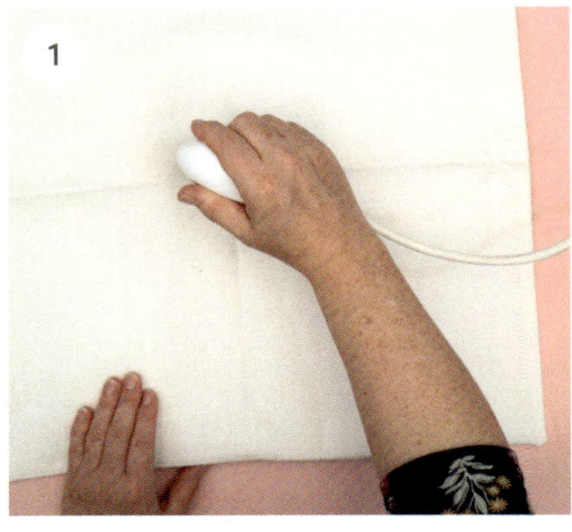

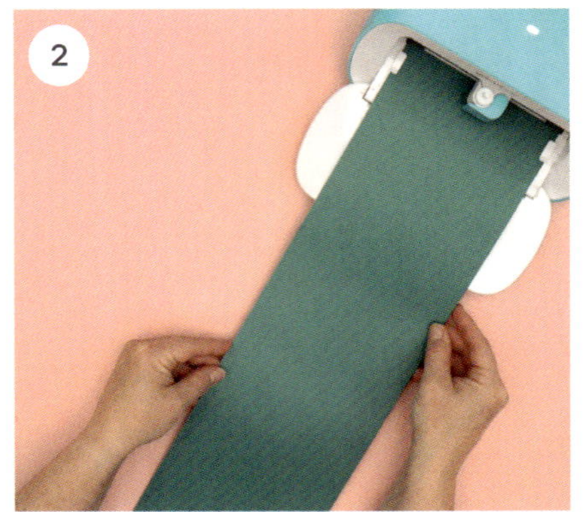

1 Unfold your pillow blank and give it a press. The EasyPress Mini is often my go-to for removing any creases in my sewing or fabric makes.

2 Access the Leaves and Berries or your chosen images from Design Space. I will be cutting the leaves in several different types of material. I just repeat the cuts for each type, and then do the same for multiple berry materials. Load any Smart Materials directly into your machine ready for cutting.

3 Add any relevant materials on to your mat and use your brayer to make sure it is air-bubble and crease free. With Infusible Ink transfer sheets you need to load them carrier sheet face-down and the matte/coloured sheet face up. You will also need to remember to use the 'Mirror' function in Design Space for Infusible Ink. The leaves and berries look the same whichever way around, but it's important to remember this if you're creating a design with a specific direction, such as text.

4 Follow the on-screen instructions for cutting the designs and load the materials when requested.

5 Weed each layer of your design. When you weed any Infusible Ink layers, the thick paper-style transfer sheet sort of 'cracks' off the carrier sheet. Make sure you pull up gently and carefully so that the paper does not tear.

6 Repeat with your other material types if using multiple different colours and textures. I have chosen to create leaves in: Infusible Ink Transfer Sheets in Watercolour Green and Bright Green; Everyday Iron-On in Kelly Green and Grass Green; Metallic Iron-On in Rose Gold; Glitter Iron-On in Mint and Kelly Green.

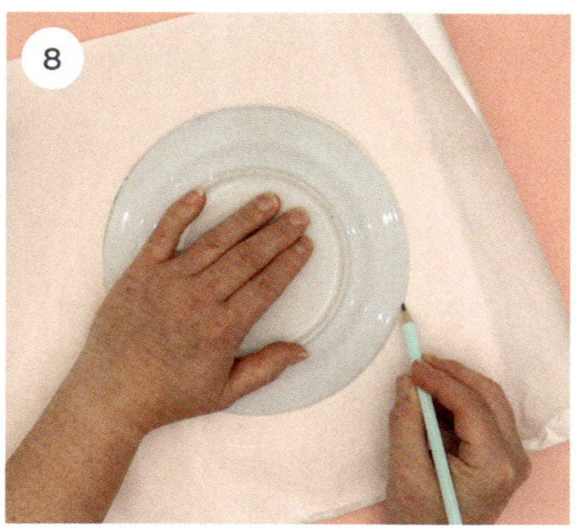

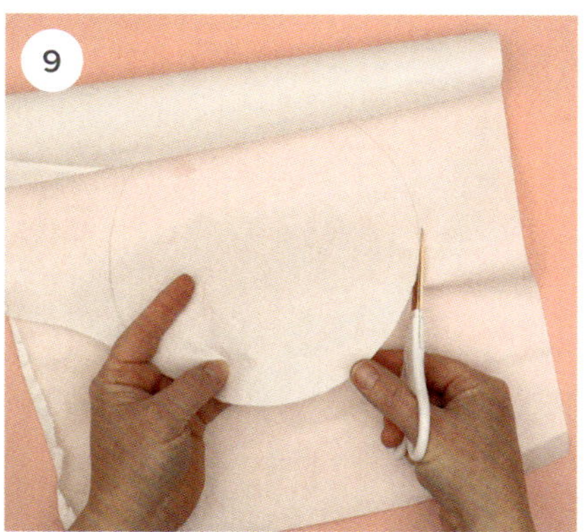

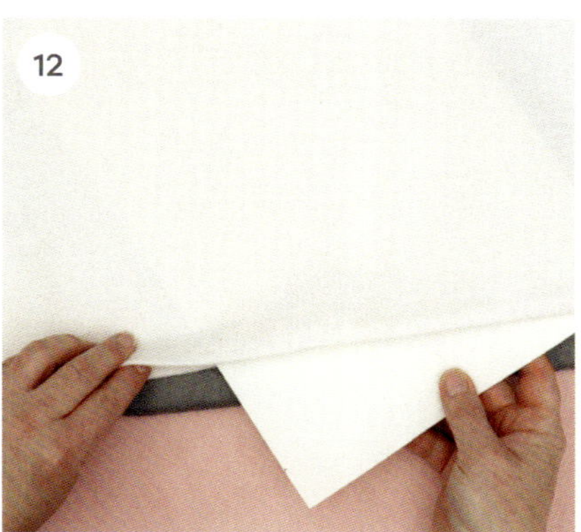

7 Repeat with your berries. I have chosen to create berries in: Infusible Ink in Cherry Red; Metallic Iron-On in Red; Glitter Iron-On in Red.

8 To help guide your leaves into a circular wreath shape you need to create a circular template. Take a spare piece of the Butcher Paper or an ordinary piece of paper and a small side plate (or anything else round) and draw around this using your pencil. Or use a compass to create a circle.

9 Cut out your template using your scissors.

10 Take note which side and where the cushion zip is before you get creating on to the cushion. I have decided to have the zip at the bottom.

11 You will be able to use your template as you go along to make sure your wreath remains approximately circular and also central to the cushion blank. Your wreath doesn't need to be 'perfect' – it is depicting wild leaves – but it does help as a guide.

12 Take another sheet of the Butcher Paper or a thick piece of card and place inside the cushion. This limits the possibility of your Infusible Ink transferring through to the other side.

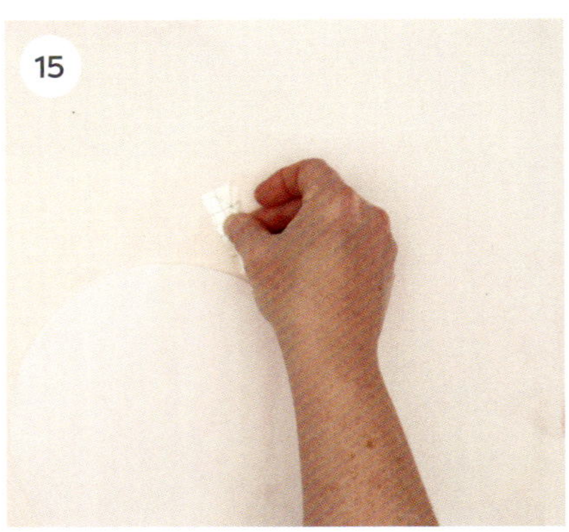

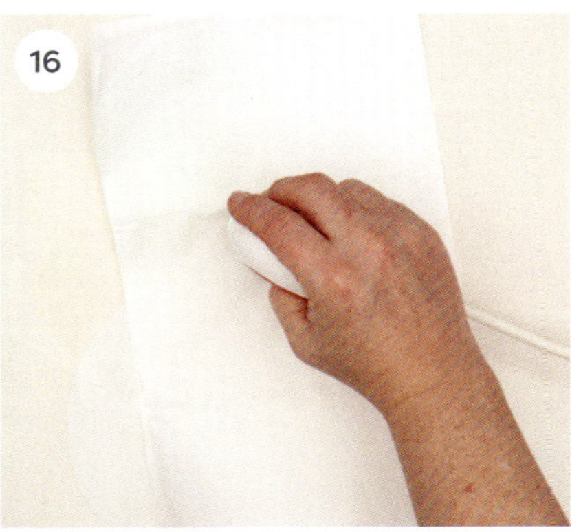

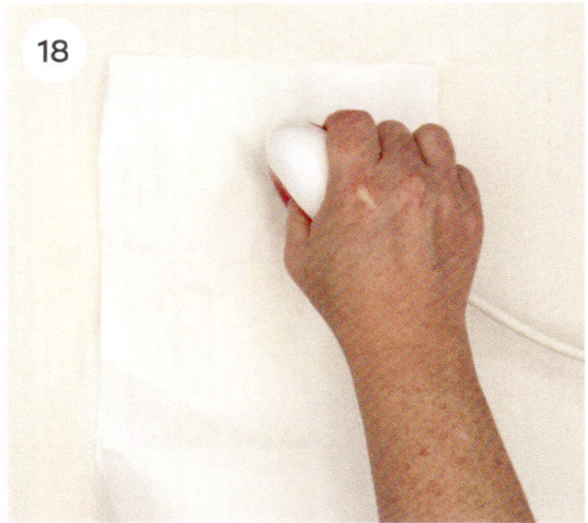

13 Cut individual leaves and berries out using your scissors so they are ready to apply to your cushion.

14 I find it easiest to make a little pile of each size and type of leaf, so I can make sure it's easy to see when layering up a variety of the greens and textures.

15 Start with any Infusible Ink leaves on the bottom layer of your wreath design. Check the Cricut Heat Guide for the latest advice on what temperature and time settings are recommended for your chosen materials and your EasyPress version. Place the first leaf on to your cushion, using your circular template as the guide. The sticky carrier sheet should help you to position this where you want.

16 Place another piece of the Butcher Paper on top before following the heat and timing instructions for application. Be careful to keep the EasyPress flat.

17 Allow your Infusible Ink sheet to cool fully before peeling away.

18 Add another Infusible Ink leaf next to your first one before heating in the same way to transfer. I have chosen to mix up the greens and the leaf sizes here.

19 You may find that some of the ink colour from the first leaf transfers slightly on to your Butcher Paper, so be careful if you're using the paper again. Try to use a clean area or piece of paper each time for each transfer.

20 Allow to cool, before peeling away.

21 Start to add variety to your leaves by overlapping the different iron-on materials. You can layer Everyday Iron-On on to Infusible Ink, then the 'Speciality' Iron-Ons like Glitter and Metallic. If you try to layer Everyday on to Glitter Iron-on it is unlikely to adhere properly! Heat each new layer at a time. Just peel back any carrier sheet in the way. Add your new leaves before replacing any other carrier-sheet pieces to protect everything. For any surrounding iron-on materials, make sure you leave any carrier sheets in position until you have finished the section you are working on.

NOTE The heating times may vary for the different iron-on materials so make sure to check these, and you may need to adjust or heat again.

22 Start working your way around in a circular pattern, continuing to overlap the different leaf types and keeping them in the same direction. Use Butcher Paper on top for any Infusible Ink transfers and keep the carrier sheet on until all heating is finished for the iron-on transfers. Try not to create too many layers of iron-on in one section or everything can become quite rigid and the fabric loses its flexibility.

23 Move the piece of card inside the cushion, if necessary, to wherever you are heating so the colour doesn't transfer out to the back of your cushion.

24 Remember to add in some little berries in the same way.

19

20

21

22

23

24

25 Continue working your way around the wreath.

26 You can always go back and add to a previous section if you feel it needs it, but be careful to make sure to cover any previously transferrec parts to protect them from damage.

27 To make sure the wreath is even, I find it helpful to line the template into position.

28 Once you are done, remove the piece of card or Butcher Paper from inside your cushion.

29 And you are done! A lovely, festive, berry-filled wreath cushion design.

GOING BEYOND THE MAKE

This technique and design could also look great on the Cricut bottle bag blank. You could also coordinate your festive décor with the Paper Leaf Wreath project on page 88. The Cricut pillow blank is specifically designed to work with Infusible Ink, but you could replicate this project design using iron-on vinyl on any cushion blank. It would look lovely with paler green leaves and white berries.

Lunchbox Stickers

My son Rupert LOVES stickers. I do too! I love how they can be simply used to make pictures, to craft and to decorate. When Cricut released products to make your own stickers, this was absolutely incredible. And these ones are even waterproof! This project uses the 'Print Then Cut' function, which also requires the use of an inkjet printer. However, if you have access to one of these, the sticker world is ready for whatever you would like to create.

YOU WILL NEED

MACHINE

- Cricut Machine and Blade (I used Cricut Joy Xtra and Fine Point Blade for Cricut Joy Xtra)

TOOLS

- Cricut StandardGrip Mat (if required)
- Cricut Brayer
- Cricut Scraper
- Cricut Spatula
- Inkjet Printer

MATERIALS

- Cricut Printable Waterproof Sticker Set, Transparent (A4/letter-sized)
- Lunchbox and/or Water Bottle (they need to have a smooth surface)

IMAGES

- Design Space Tractor SVG #M4905F740

NOTES

- Select a sticker-compatible machine, as not all of the machines can do this project.
- Make sure your machine has been sticker calibrated. The first time you make stickers it may ask you to do this, so follow the on-screen Design Space instructions. This will ensure your machine is accurate when cutting your sticker designs.
- Instead of the 'Transparent' Waterproof Sticker Set, you may prefer to make this in another variant, such as the 'White' or 'Holographic' versions. It depends on how you would like your stickers to be and what you are applying them to.
- I am using my Tractor image in Design Space for this project. You could use this technique with whatever image you like.

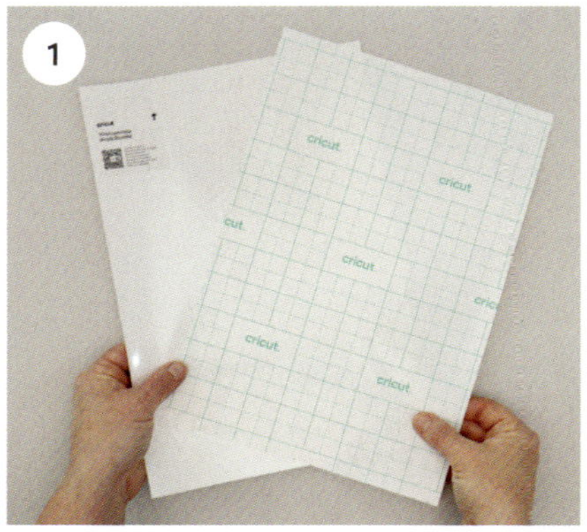

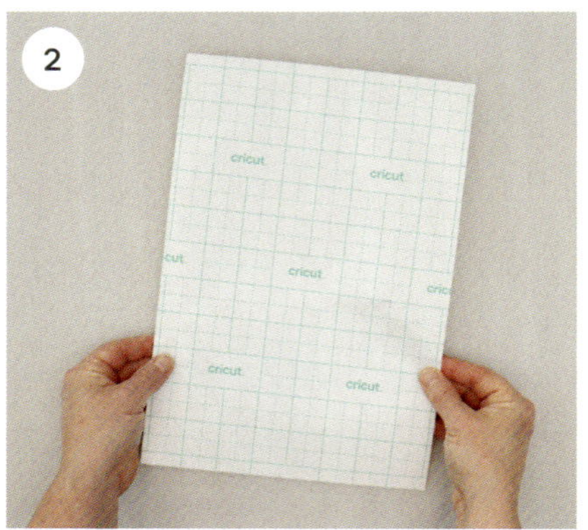

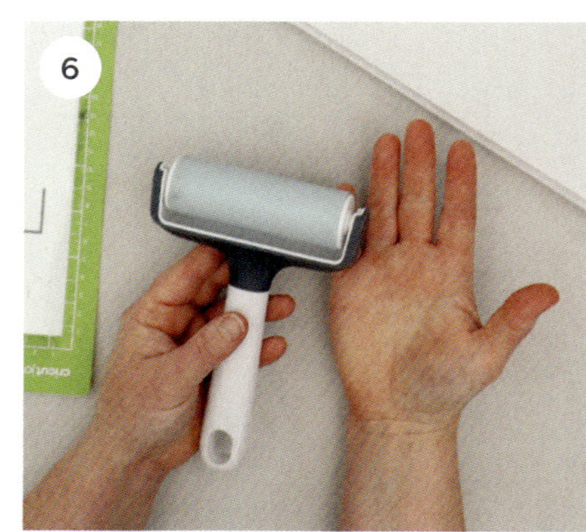

1 Access the Tractor or your chosen image from Design Space. You will initially need your Printable Waterproof Sticker Set and your inkjet printer.

2 Convert the Tractor SVG from 'Cut' function to a 'Print Then Cut' function in Design Space. Duplicate it as many times as you like. I have also changed the size of some of the tractors to allow for some large and some small. Follow the on-screen instructions for printing your stickers with your inkjet printer. Make sure to test which way up your printer prints and then load your sticker sheet accordingly. The back of the sheet is the one with the grid on, including the Cricut logo.

3 Once printed out, it will also include black marks around the edges. These are 'registration marks' that help your machine scan and guide it where to cut out.

4 Line your printed sticker sheet on to your mat, in the top left-hand corner.

5 Use your brayer to make sure everything is stuck down securely.

6 Be careful of any printer ink transferring to your brayer or hands.

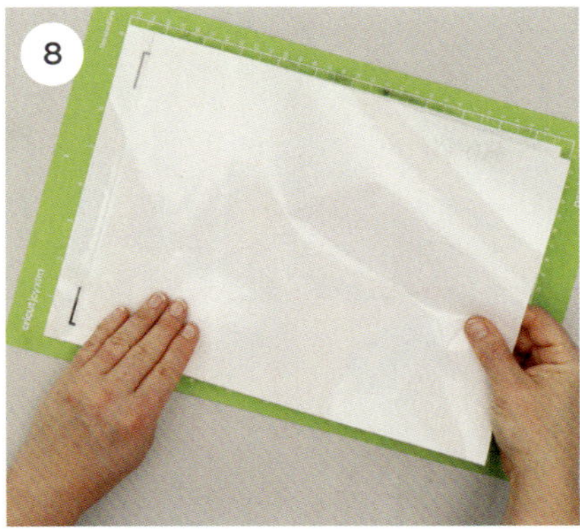

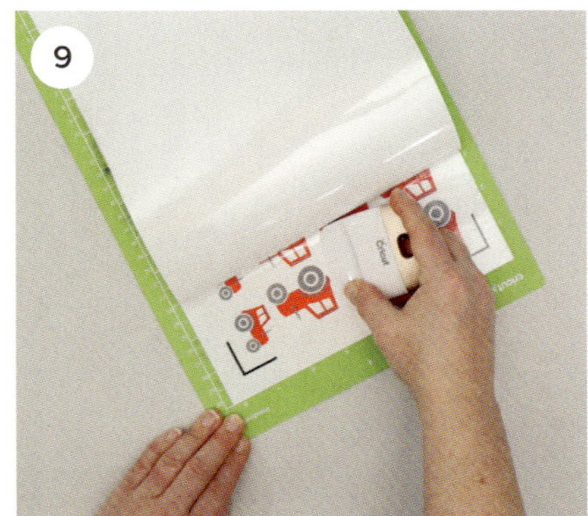

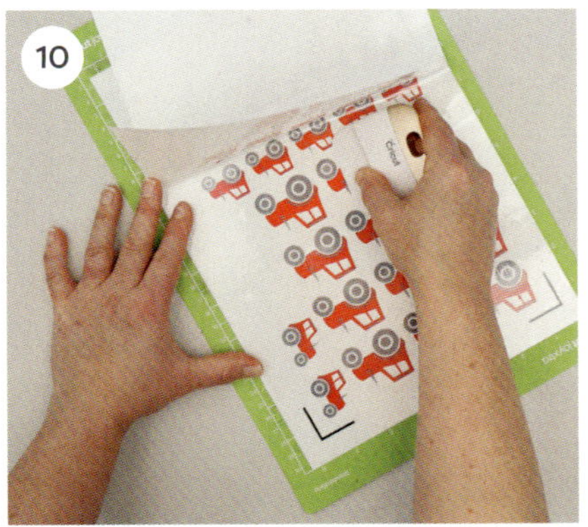

7 Tear the small strip off the top of the laminate sheet.

8 Line up the sticky part of the laminate sheet with the top of the printed sheet. Ideally you only want to do this once, so try to make sure they are lined up correctly.

9 Using your scraper, push the laminate down on to your printed sheet. Go slowly, moving your scraper from side to side to ensure all air bubbles are pushed out and everything is nice and smooth.

10 Continue until all of the carrier sheet is removed, and the laminate sheet is fully stuck down on to your sticker sheet.

11 Follow the on-screen instructions for your stickers to be cut out. Your machine will likely spend some time initially scanning to make sure everything is lined up.

12 Once cut, unload the mat before peeling back your sticker sheet.

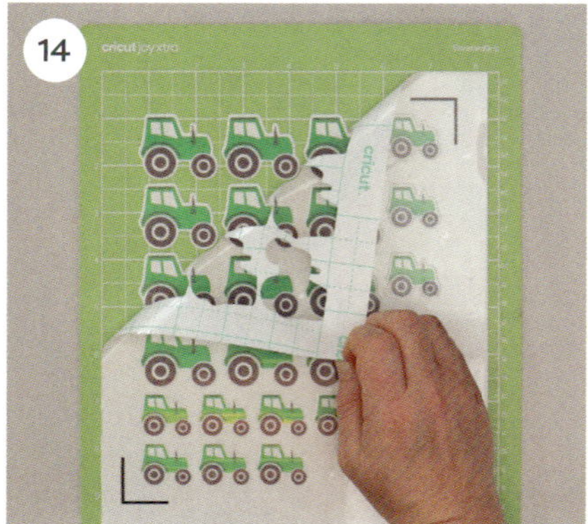

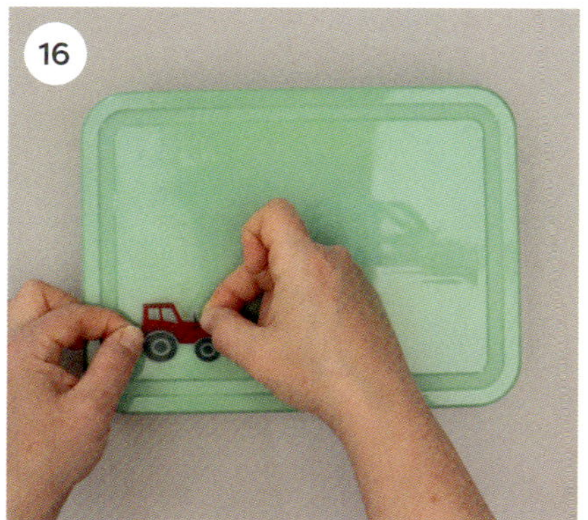

13 You may find the spatula helpful to remove the sheet from the mat.

14 I chose these stickers to be 'Kiss Cut', which means that the machine has cut the sticker sheet only, leaving the carrier sheet intact. If you choose the 'Die Cut' option, your machine will also cut through the carrier sheet, so you will have individual stickers.

NOTE: It is important that you ensure your inkjet printer has plenty of ink for your designs or you will end up with lines across your images. Even if this happens, I would still recommend making and keeping these stickers – you may still have a use for them and it feels a waste to just bin them. I have given these tractor ones to my son, Rupert, to play with. While it feels a waste of my original sticker plan, they are still being used and loved!

15 Now we are ready to start transferring the stickers to the lunchbox. Make sure everything is clean, dry and dust free before proceeding. As these are 'Kiss Cut' stickers, simply peel off each sticker from the carrier sheet...

16 ...before sticking down wherever you like!

17 Use the scraper to make sure the sticker is nice and smoothly applied and air-bubble free.

18 Continue to add stickers. I have chosen to add these tractors in a nice row, which I have then repeated on the opposite side.

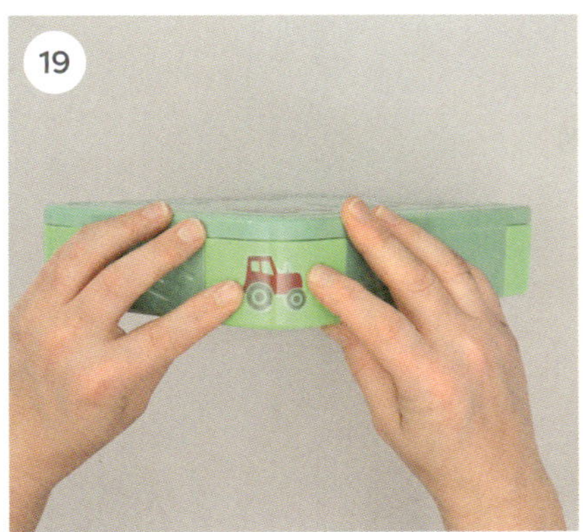

19 You can apply stickers to curved surfaces as well, just make sure to smooth everything out as before. I have added smaller versions of the tractors to each curved corner.

20 Repeat the same process on your water bottle.

21 And you are done! The transparent stickers will stand out more against an opaque background, such as on this lunchbox. When added to a clear surface, such as the water bottle, you will be able to see all the way through, which gives the printed image a slightly more subtle finish. Wait 24–48 hours before contact with water to allow the vinyl to be fully fixed. I would recommend hand washing these only.

MORE IDEAS

These daisies have been made in the same way, but using White sticker paper instead of Transparent. You can see how they stand out against the translucent water bottle. This Daisy design can be found in Cricut Design Space under my profile with #M432FCB49.

GOING BEYOND THE MAKE

This tractor design would look lovely made in vinyl and applied to cushions, T-shirts or in fact anything you like (perhaps as a fun addition to kitchen aprons such as the project on page 108). This waterproof sticker material would be great to decorate outdoor signs or even car bumpers.

Wooden Weather Magnets

Can you believe that Cricut Maker can cut WOOD? It is this kind of project that makes me feel like they really are magic crafty machines. These cute weather shapes would look lovely on an office magnet board or to hang up mementos and reminders on your kitchen fridge. You could create more clouds, lightning and raindrops too if you wanted to create a larger weather magnet system!

YOU WILL NEED

MACHINE

- Cricut Machine and Blade (I used Cricut Maker 3 and Cricut Knife Blade)

TOOLS

- Cricut StrongGrip Mat
- Cricut Brayer
- Cricut Weeder
- Cricut Scissors
- Glue Gun
- Paint Palette
- Paintbrush

MATERIALS

- Cricut Basswood
- Cricut Permanent Yellow Vinyl
- Masking Tape
- Acrylic Paint
- Magnets

IMAGES

- Exclusive Sunshine SVG
- Exclusive Circle SVG
- Exclusive Clouds SVG
- Exclusive Lightning SVG
- Exclusive Raindrops SVG

NOTES

- It is really important to use the StrongGrip Mat on this project to make sure the wood does not move around during cutting. And don't skip the masking tape step as this also makes sure the wood does not move around.
- The exclusive SVG files are all coloured on the original files, but you need to make everything (except for the sunshine) the same colour on the Canvas so that Design Space cuts them all at once onto your basswood piece. We will cut the sunshine shape later from vinyl.
- Your machine may take quite a while to cut the thicker wood materials so plan this make for when you have a decent length of time to allow the machine to work its cutting magic.

1 Upload your images to your Canvas in Design Space. Add your basswood to the mat and use your brayer to ensure everything is firmly in position.

2 Add masking tape along all four sides of your basswood. Make sure the tape is quite near the edge of the wood and that the shapes to be cut do not go through the masking tape. Position accordingly in Design Space.

3 Did you know that the little white star wheels on your machine track can move? It is really important that you gently slide these to the right-hand side before you begin cutting or your thick wood will be marked.

4 You may find that your design cuts over several 'passes'. The knife blade will need to repeat the same shape over and over again until the material has been cut all the way through. Don't be tempted to cancel the cut when you think it has been completed. You may find that while it appears to be done, it may not be.

NOTE At the end of the cutting, Design Space will likely ask you to 'check' your cut. Do this without unloading your mat or moving the wood in any way. If you need to cut again, the blade will repeat the shapes exactly. Using your weeder, try and gently remove one of the smaller pieces. If you find it is still connected, repeat the cut so you can be sure the wood has been cut all the way through. If you find the wood is only slightly connected, you could remove the shapes and finish cutting the edges using your scissors.

5 Once your shapes are fully cut out, remove your masking tape from around the edge of your basswood.

6 Peel back the basswood from your mat.

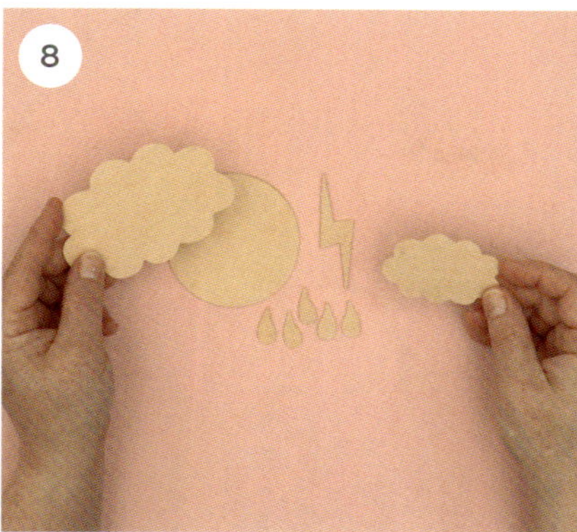

7 Gently take out your shapes.

8 If there are any edges that have loose fibres or rough parts, use your scissors or some sandpaper to tidy them.

9 You are now ready to get painting! You will need your paint, a paintbrush and a paint palette. I have put some scrap paper underneath to protect my work surface. I have chosen to use matte acrylic paint in a variety of colours. I have used white and grey for the clouds, blue for raindrops and yellow for the lightning.

10 Paint the larger circle a darker blue for the sky. You will apply the yellow vinyl sunshine on to this later.

11 I have chosen to paint both sides of the wooden pieces, but you could just paint one side if you prefer. Allow your painted wooden pieces to dry.

12 You may be wondering why I didn't make the sunshine in wood. I have tried this before but I found that the smaller, fiddly shapes often split or crack. I tried making the sunshine in wood to show you what can happen, and I was right. The smaller sunshine rays were just too delicate and snapped when trying to remove the shape from the main basswood piece. I think making the sunshine in glossy Permanent Vinyl works well in contrast to the bright matte blue paint.

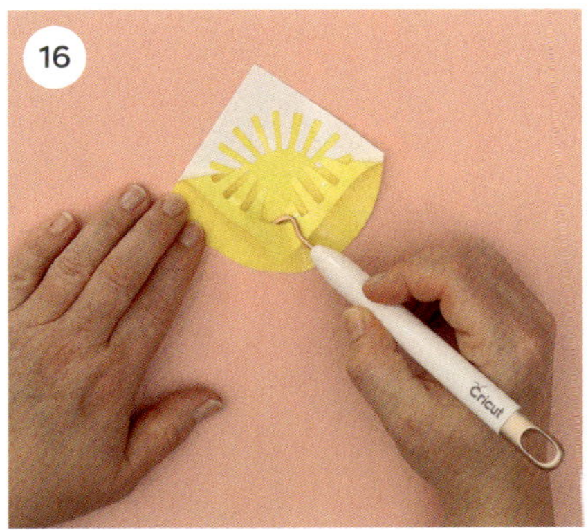

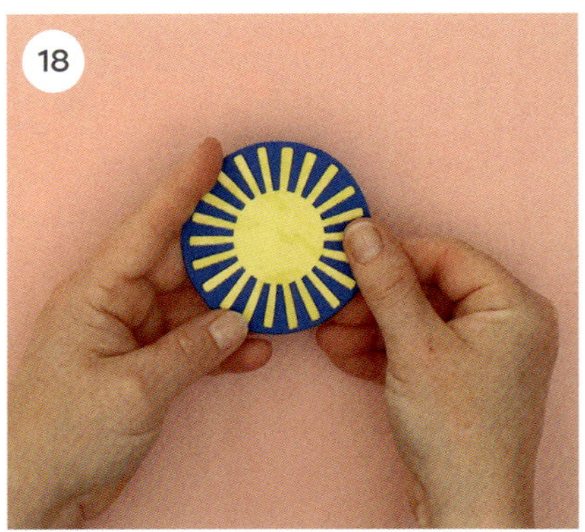

13 Add your vinyl to your mat. I wouldn't always use a StrongGrip Mat for the vinyl. I would swap out for a StandardGrip. In this case, I have used this StrongGrip mat several times, so it has slightly less stickiness. I have not used a brayer this time as it has stuck down enough and is smooth and air-bubble free.

14 Load your mat and follow the on-screen instructions for cutting out your vinyl sunshine.

15 Trim around your design, reserving any leftover vinyl for future projects.

16 Weed out your sunshine design.

17 Gently peel your sunshine away from the carrier sheet. The sun rays are quite delicate, so go slowly to try and ensure they do not tear.

18 Take your painted blue circle of wood and place your vinyl sunshine in the middle.

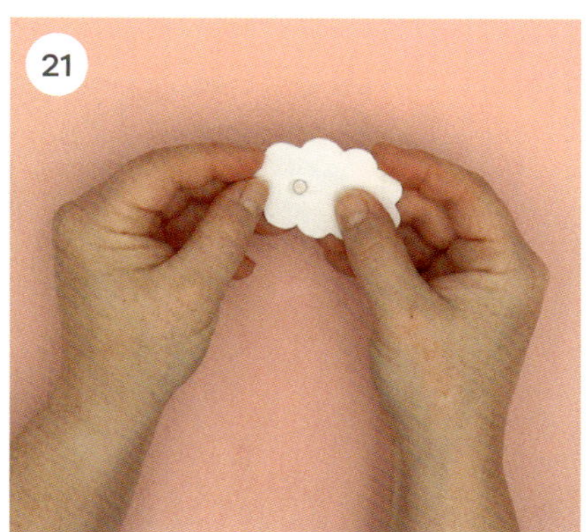

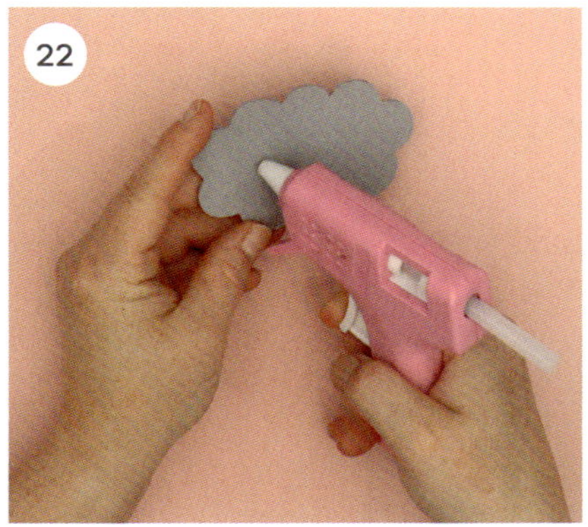

19 We are now ready to turn your wooden shapes into magnets. Select your small magnets and glue gun.

20 Add a small piece of hot glue on to the back of one of your wooden shapes.

21 Push your magnet into the hot glue to secure.

22 Repeat with your other magnet shapes.

23 On the larger pieces I have chosen to add two small magnets to the back, so repeat if required.

24 And you are done! You have lovely weather-themed magnets to brighten your home.

GOING BEYOND THE MAKE

This project can only be created with machines compatible with the knife blade, but you could buy pre-cut small wooden craft shapes and personalize them with a Cricut vinyl design or font ready to convert into a magnet. Or why not try other shapes and designs in the wood too.

THE
Milner
FAMILY

Personalized Doormat

We have a vibrant pink front door in our home and I am forever trying to find the 'perfect' doormat to go with this fun colour. We have recently gone through rainbows, funny slogans and festive ones. This project utilizes simple but effective text 'The Milner Family' (my family). But once you learn how to create your own personalized doormats, trust me, it will be a new 'thing' in your life to create many. This would make a lovely gift for someone in their new home.

YOU WILL NEED

MACHINE

- Cricut Machine and Blade (I used Cricut Explore 3 and Fine Point Blade for Cricut Explore)

MATERIALS

- Cricut Stencil Vinyl
- Cricut Transfer Tape
- Blank Coir Doormat
- Acrylic Paint

TOOLS

- Cricut Brayer
- Cricut Weeder
- Cricut Tweezers
- Cricut Scissors
- Cricut Scraper
- Paint Palette
- Paintbrush
- Cricut Roll Holder (optional)

FONTS

- Cloud 9
- Cricut Sans

NOTES

- I have not used a Cricut mat here as this version of stencil vinyl is a Smart Material, but use a mat if required.
- I have chosen to use acrylic paint as it is nice and easy to apply, has a good consistency for coating easily, dries quickly and is relatively hard wearing.
- While a larger paintbrush would, of course, allow you to add more paint at a time, a smaller paintbrush takes longer but allows for greater precision and for you to add more paint within the coir texture of the mat.

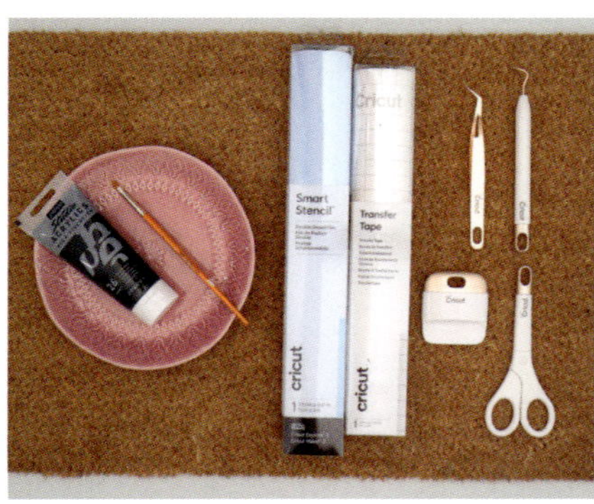

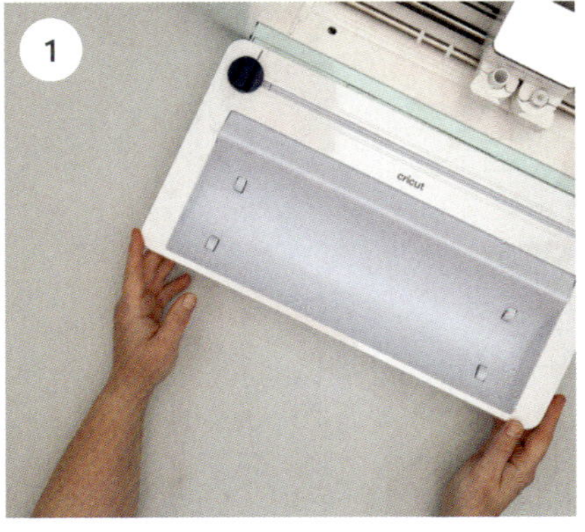

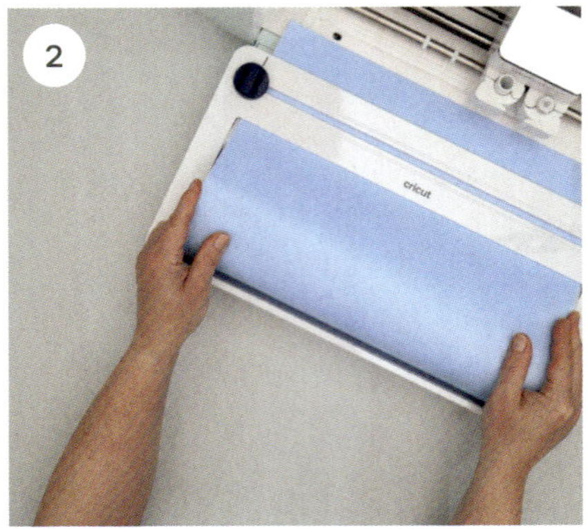

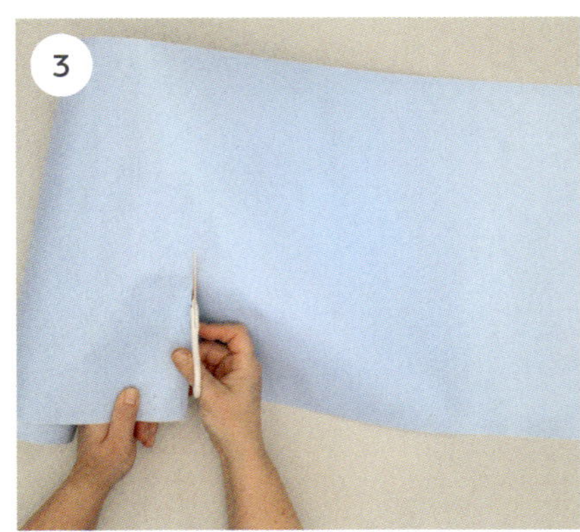

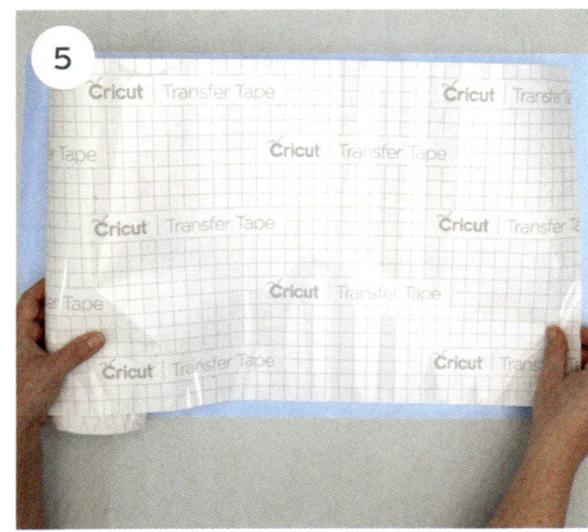

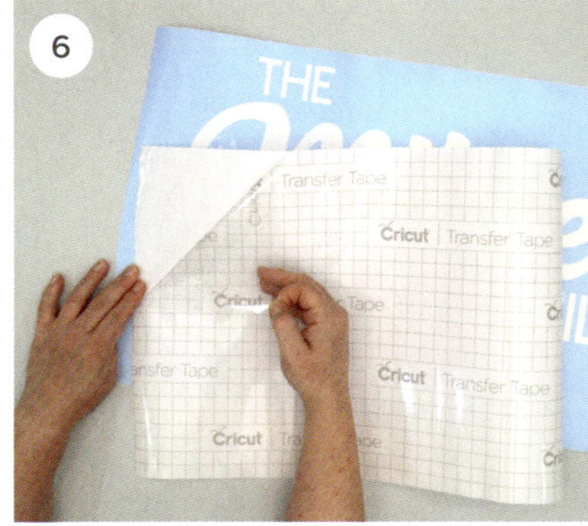

1 Choose your font and text. Make sure to measure your doormat and adjust the text size accordingly in Design Space. If choosing to use a roll holder, load it into position. I do find this tool particularly useful when using long rolls of materials.

2 Gently push your vinyl in through your roll holder or load it directly into your machine (or with a mat if that suits your project best). Follow the on-screen instructions for cutting your design.

3 Once cut, unload and use your scissors to trim back your design.

4 Weed out your design. You will need to weed out wherever you want the paint to appear on your doormat. Once you have weeded everything out, you are ready to transfer this to your doormat.

5 Cut a piece of Transfer Tape that is larger than your cut-out design.

6 Peel back the sticky tape from the carrier sheet. When working with a large piece of tape like this, be careful it doesn't fold back and get stuck to itself!

7 Gently push the Transfer Tape across your design so it is smooth and flat. Use your scraper if needed to do this.

8 Pull your vinyl and tape away from the carrier sheet.

9 Position everything on to your doormat.

10 Peel back your Transfer Tape leaving just the vinyl on your doormat. You may need to use your tweezers or a spatula for gently holding down any fiddly parts.

11 Smooth everything out to make sure it is well stuck down. You are now ready to get painting!

12 Start applying your paint inside the stencil gaps.

13 Work your way across the stencil, applying paint where it is required.

14 Once complete, leave everything in position and allow to dry. Acrylic paint dries very quickly but I left this overnight to be sure.

15 Peel back your stencil to reveal your now painted design! Keep gently pulling it all away – you may want to use tweezers to pull back any of the fiddlier parts.

16 And you are done! One lovely, personalized doormat.

GOING BEYOND THE MAKE

This is obviously a simple text-only design, but you could add in other shapes or multiple colours if preferred. The rainbow SVG file used in the Felt Banner project on page 158 would look fabulous converted into a stencil and painted on to a doormat. I do find that stencils on doormats tend to work best with simpler shapes or fonts, so that the paint can go on smoothly on to the textured coir material with clean stencil edges.

Bunting

What celebration isn't improved by bunting! I have a special 'bunting drawer' at home in various colours, for all occasions. This one is for Christmas – it is slightly smaller than I would perhaps normally make, but it looks lovely adorning a Christmas tree.

YOU WILL NEED

MACHINE

- Cricut Machine and Blade (I used Cricut Maker 3 and Cricut Rotary Blade)

TOOLS

- Cricut FabricGrip Mat
- Cricut Fabric Scissors or Cricut Hand-Held Rotary Blade
- Cricut Brayer
- Cricut Tape Measure
- Cricut Snips
- Cricut Spatula (optional)
- Cricut Weeder (optional)
- Cricut Pins and Cushion (optional)
- Cricut Seam Ripper (optional)
- Cricut Thimble (optional)
- Sewing Machine
- Cricut Cutting Mat & Ruler (optional)
- Iron or Cricut EasyPress (optional)

MATERIALS

- 100% Cotton Fabric (Print)
- 100% Cotton Fabric (Plain)
- Binding or Coordinating Fabric
- 100% Cotton Thread

IMAGES

- Design Space Basic Free Triangle Shape

NOTES

- If you do not have a fabric-cutting compatible machine, you could complete this project using your Cricut cutting mat, ruler and rotary blade. Cut out triangles before proceeding with the sewing steps.
- I have chosen to use my own 'The Crafty Lass' X Craft Cotton Co fabric range 'Berries and Blooms'. The design is called 'Garland Joy'. You could, of course, use whatever fabric you want to.

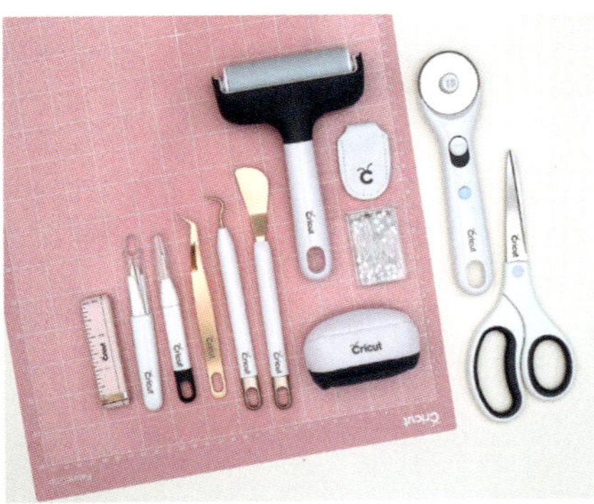

1 Using your fabric scissors or rotary blade, trim your fabric to the right size for your fabric mat.

2 Use your brayer to attach the fabric on to your mat. Make sure there aren't any air bubbles or ridges in your fabric.

3 Add a triangle to your Design Space Canvas and duplicate as necessary. I cut 24 triangles around 3in (7.5cm) X 4½in (11.5cm) as they fit nicely together on the 24in (60cm) mat. Load your fabric-loaded mat into your machine when requested and follow the on-screen instructions for cutting.

4 Once cut, unload your mat and weed away the bits between your triangles. You can gently pull these away or use the weeder, if necessary.

5 Pull your triangles from the mat – you may find your spatula useful for this.

6 Repeat with the same size and quantity of triangles in the fabric for the back of your bunting triangles.

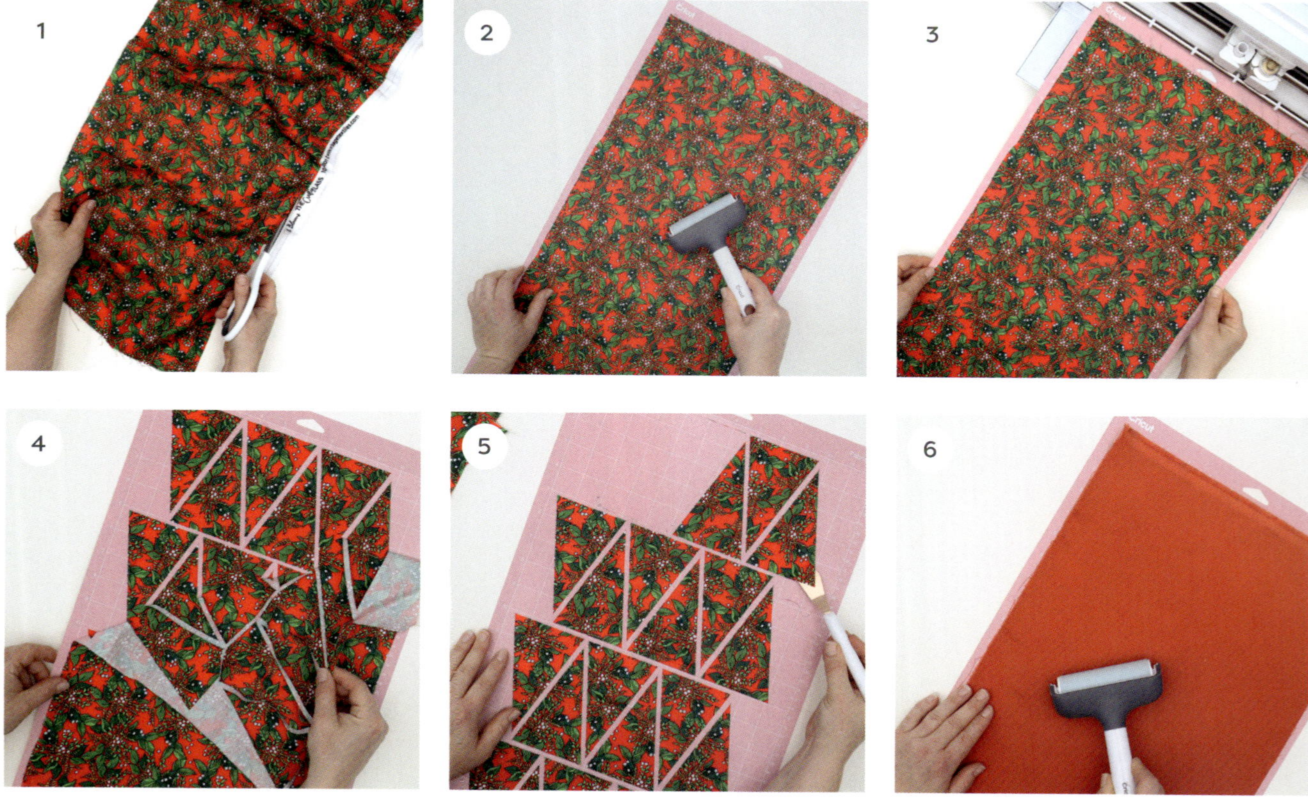

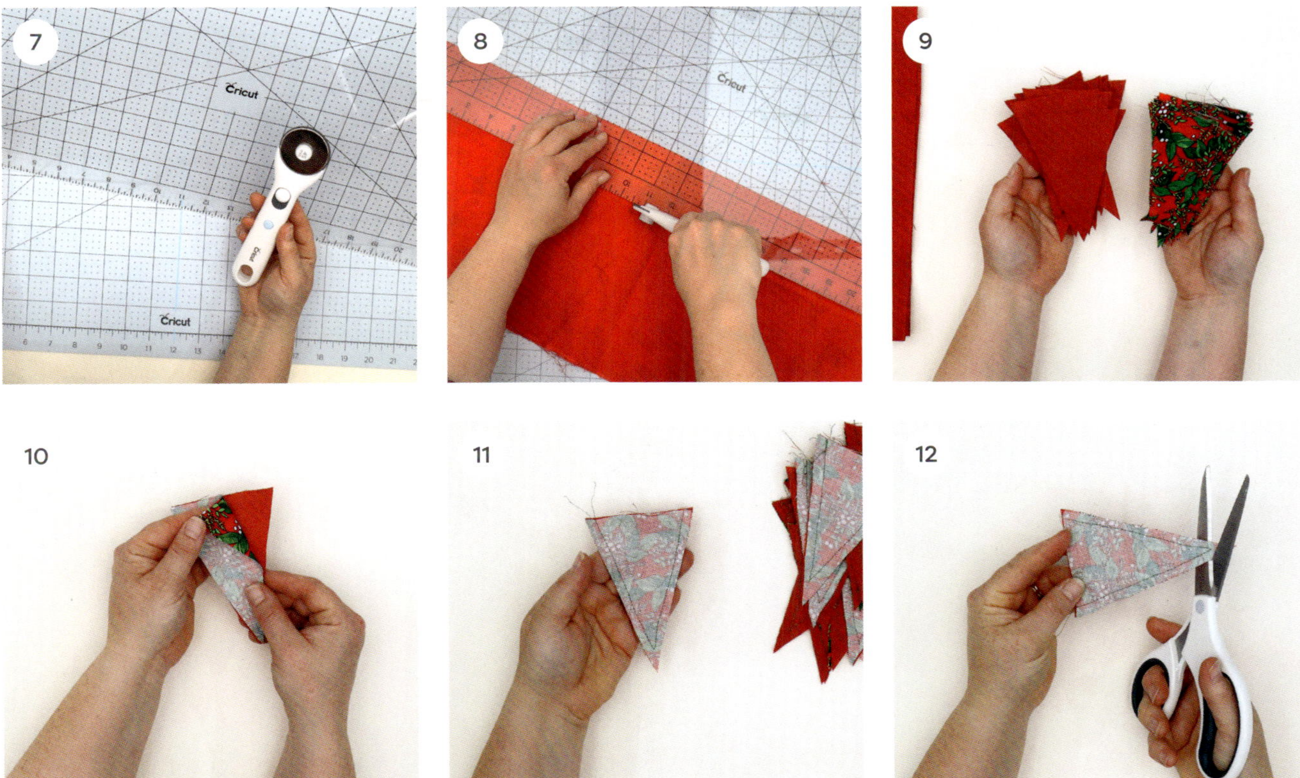

7 If you have pre-made binding, please skip to step 9. Otherwise, select your cutting mat, ruler and rotary blade.

8 Cut 2½in (6.3cm) wide lengths in your coordinating fabric. You may need to join some together to make the correct length for your bunting.

9 You should now have triangles for the front, triangles for the back and your binding.

10 Place a front and back triangle right sides together.

11 Using a simple running stitch, sew down one long side, pivot, and back up the other side. Secure your threads. Repeat with your other triangles.

12 Trim away any excess fabric at the very tip of your bunting triangle.

13 Turn your triangle out the right way. Make sure to push your triangle completely out. You may be able to do this as it is, or a 'pointy' tool such as a Cricut stylus is very useful for this.

14 Trim your threads and any excess fabric at the top so everything is neat. Repeat steps 10 to 14 with the rest of your triangles.

15 You will now need your binding. If you have pre-made binding it should already be pressed. If you have made your own use an iron or EasyPress to crease. I fold the bias binding in half widthways and press, before folding each outside edge inwards so the raw edges meet in the middle and are concealed inside.

16 Place one of your bunting triangles inside the binding. Remember to leave a small gap at the end of the binding to have somewhere to tie your bunting up.

17 Pin your bunting triangle into position and repeat with your other triangles, keeping the distance between each one the same.

18 You are now ready to sew along your binding, securing your triangles inside. You could use a simple running stitch as we did to create the triangles, or choose a more decorative one – the choice is up to you! Remove your pins as you go. Secure your threads, and you are finished! Ready to hang up or adorn your Christmas tree.

GOING BEYOND THE MAKE

The simple triangle shape is also used as an effective design for the Fiesta Table Mats on page 76. There are further fabric projects: Reusable Face Wipes on page 154 and the Patchwork Cushion on page 164.

While cutting some sewing projects with a rotary cutter can be more suitable, Cricut Maker makes for precise, quick and perfect cuts every time (particularly for multiple duplicated shapes). Why not cut out fabric shapes for a quilt?

Reusable Face Wipes

Create these soft and reusable face wipes using brushed cotton alongside some pretty cotton prints. If you do not have a fabric-cutting compatible machine, you could complete this project using your Cricut cutting mat, ruler and rotary blade.

YOU WILL NEED

MACHINE

- Cricut Machine and Blade (I used Cricut Maker 3 and Cricut Rotary Blade)

TOOLS

- Cricut FabricGrip Mat
- Cricut Fabric Scissors or Cricut Hand-Held Rotary Blade
- Cricut Brayer
- Cricut Tape Measure
- Cricut Snips
- Cricut Spatula (optional)
- Cricut Weeder (optional)
- Cricut Pins and Cushion (optional)
- Cricut Seam Ripper (optional)
- Cricut Thimble (optional)
- Cricut Cutting Mat & Ruler
- Sewing Machine
- Iron or Cricut EasyPress (optional)

MATERIALS

- 100% Cotton (Prints)
- 100% Brushed Cotton (Grey)
- 100% Cotton Thread

IMAGES

- Design Space Basic Free Square Shape

NOTES

- If you do not have a fabric-cutting compatible machine you need to cut 3½in (9cm) squares before proceeding with the sewing steps.
- Instead of brushed cotton, you could use soft jersey, bamboo cotton or other equivalent soft fabrics.

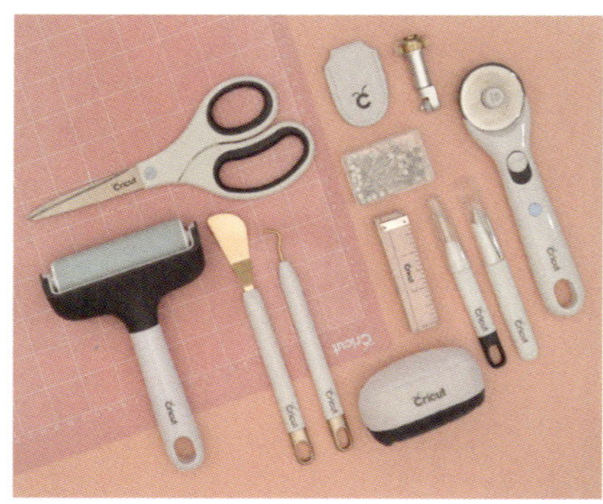

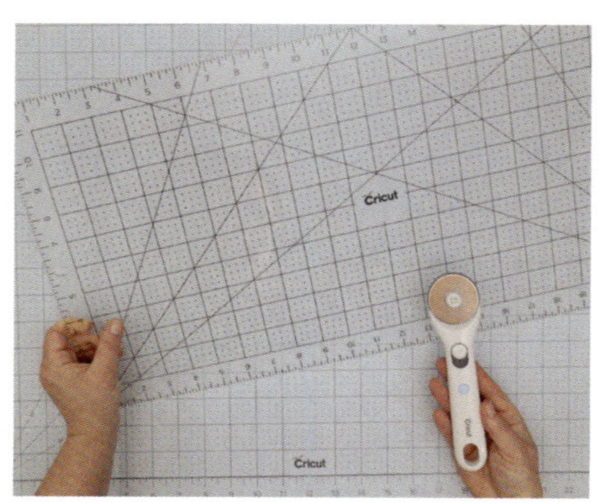

1 Using your fabric scissors or hand-held rotary blade cut a 12in (30.5cm) square ready to attach on to your fabric mat. Press if required.

2 Use your brayer to attach the fabric on to your mat. Make sure there aren't any air bubbles or ridges in your fabric.

3 Add a 3½in (9cm) square to your Design Space Canvas and duplicate as necessary. I have cut 9 squares in total per fabric colour as they fit nicely on to the 12in (30.5cm) mat. Load your fabric-loaded mat into your machine when requested and follow the on-screen instructions.

4 Once cut, unload your mat and weed away the bits between your squares. You can gently pull these away or use your weeder, if necessary. Pull your squares from the mat. Repeat if you want to make in different coloured fabrics.

5 Repeat with your brushed cotton. You will need one brushed cotton square for every printed cotton square, so repeat as many times as necessary.

6 Select one brushed cotton square and one printed cotton square.

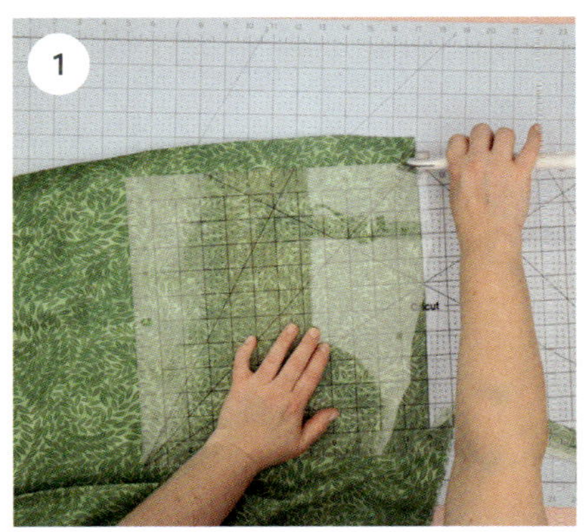

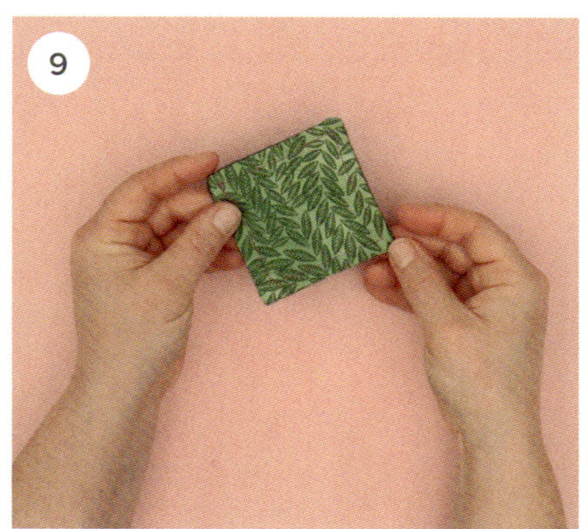

7 Place together, right sides together, although some brushed cotton is the same on both sides. Using your sewing machine, sew around the edges leaving a gap for turning out. It helps to do some backward stitches at the beginning and end to make it nice and secure.

8 Open up the gap and turn your sewn square the right way out. Push out the corners. You can do this using your fingers, or another tool if preferred. The scoring stylus is a helpful tool for this!

9 Once you have pressed all of the corners out, flatten your square down ready for sewing again. Sew all the way around the edge using a straight running stitch. You could also use a decorative embroidery-style stitch, depending on your machine. Just so long as your turning gap is now secure and closed.

10 Repeat with your other squares and colours.

11 And you are done! Some lovely, reusable face wipes.

GOING BEYOND THE MAKE

These fabric face wipes would make a lovely gift – perhaps you could add some inside the Anemone Cosmetics Bag project on page 114.

Using your cutting machine to cut squares (and other shapes) is really useful for sewing projects such as quilting.

Freddie & Rupert
CREATE YOUR OWN
RAINBOW

Rainbow Felt Banner

★ ★

My boys both absolutely love rainbows and this colourful banner will look brilliant hanging up in their playroom! The felt adds some lovely texture to the make. You could personalize the name and message around this exclusively designed funky rainbow.

YOU WILL NEED

MACHINES

- Cricut Machine and Blade (I used Cricut Maker 3 and Cricut Rotary Blade)
- Cricut EasyPress Mini

TOOLS

- Cricut FabricGrip Mat
- Cricut StandardGrip Mat
- Cricut Fabric Scissors
- Cricut Weeder
- Cricut Scissors
- Cricut Brayer
- Cricut Spatula (optional)
- Cricut Tweezers (optional)
- Cricut Scraper (optional)
- Cricut EasyPress Mat
- Glue Gun

MATERIALS

- Cricut Carousel Felt Pack
- Cricut Iron-On (your choice of colours)
- Cricut Metallic Iron-On
- 100% Cotton Calico Banner

IMAGES

- Exclusive Rainbow SVG
- Design Space Basic Free Star Shape

FONTS

- BTC Fashion Statement
- BFC Aloma Island

NOTES

- You may find it better to use the standard fine-point machine blade. It just depends on the thickness of your felt. Personally, I find the rotary blade a much better choice as it slides over the surface of the felt rather than tearing through the material.
- You may prefer to cut your text in one colour, but I have chosen to use a mix of metallic iron-on and smaller scraps in rainbow colours for the word 'RAINBOW'.
- You could use a larger EasyPress to attach the font and stars to the banner. However, using the smaller EasyPress Mini allows for greater flexibility in where you apply the heat.

1 Take your FabricGrip Mat and one of your felt sheets. Use your brayer to make sure it is securely stuck in position.

2 Upload the Rainbow SVG file and add any text you would like to your Design Space Canvas. Follow the on-screen instructions for cutting your felt out.

3 Repeat steps 1 and 2 with your other felt colour sheets. Using your weeder, weed each layer away from your FabricGrip Mat, reserving any spare felt for future crafting projects.

4 Take your StandardGrip Mat and add any vinyl you want to cut on to your mat. Load the mat and follow the on-screen instructions for cutting your iron-on.

5 Trim back your iron-on around your cut-out designs.

6 Using your weeder, weed out your designs. Using your scissors, trim out your text so everything will be ready to apply.

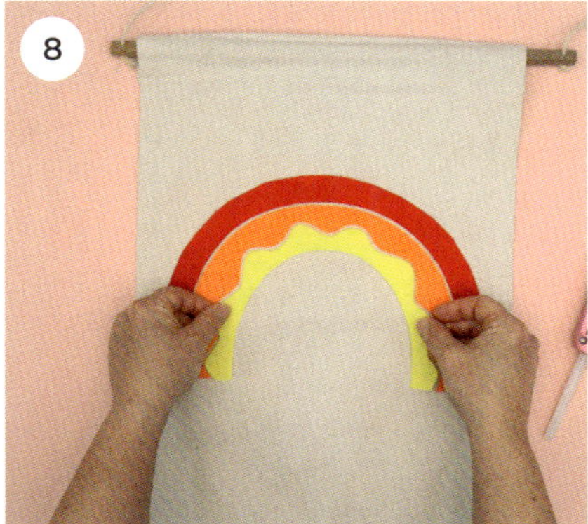

7 Now apply your felt rainbow pieces. Take your hot glue gun and apply small dabs to the back of your red rainbow piece before placing centrally on to your banner.

8 Continue with your other rainbow felt places, applying them in the same way with your hot glue gun.

9 And your rainbow is done!

10 Now select your EasyPress Mat and your EasyPress Mini. Turn on your EasyPress. It will need a small amount of time to heat up. Check the Cricut Heat Guide for the latest advice on what temperature and time settings are recommended for your chosen materials and your EasyPress version. Preheat wherever you plan to add your text.

11 Place your text into position. I have started with 'Freddie & Rupert' straight under the rainbow.

12 Use your EasyPress Mini to transfer your iron-on into position.

13 Continue with any more text you want to add. Here I have added 'Create Your Own' underneath my sons' names.

14 Lay out your 'Rainbow' text. You may need to heat each letter individually to make sure they transfer correctly and you don't trap any of the carrier sheet in the iron-on. Cover each letter with the carrier sheet while heating to protect the iron-on surface.

15 Finally, position any stars you would like around the banner.

16 Heat them into position.

17 Peel back the carrier sheet pieces and check to make sure everything is attached to the fabric banner securely.

18 And you are done! One super bright, rainbow banner.

GOING BEYOND THE MAKE

This rainbow design would look fab in iron-on in a much larger size for a cushion or much smaller on a T-shirt pocket. I would also love to see this created in stencil form for the Personalized Doormat project on page 142, or cut out in wood to co-ordinate with the Wooden Weather Magnets project on page 136.

Patchwork Cushion

This project uses English Paper Piecing (EPP) to create perfect hexagons. It is certainly less complicated than it may first appear. I quickly established that using my Cricut machine was a match made in heaven for this craft.

YOU WILL NEED

MACHINE

- Cricut Machine and Blade (I used Cricut Maker 3, Cricut Rotary Blade and Cricut FIne-Point Maker Blade)
- Fabric Glue
- Sewing Machine
- Cricut Cutting Mat & Ruler (optional)
- Iron or Cricut EasyPress (optional)

TOOLS

- Cricut FabricGrip Mat
- Cricut StandardGrip Mat
- Cricut Fabric Scissors or Cricut Hand-Held Rotary Blade
- Cricut Brayer
- Cricut Tape Measure
- Cricut Snips
- Sewing Needle
- Cricut Spatula (optional)
- Cricut Weeder (optional)
- Cricut Pins (optional)
- Cricut Seam Ripper (optional)
- Cricut Thimble (optional)

MATERIALS

- Medium-Weight Cardstock
- 100% Cotton Fabric (a mix of prints)
- Coordinating Backing Fabric
- 100% Cotton Thread
- Cushion Inner

IMAGES

- Design Space Basic Free Hexagon Shape

NOTES

- If you do not have a fabric-cutting machine, you could of course complete this project using your Cricut machine to create the paper templates before hand-cutting your fabric hexagons.
- I have chosen to use a mix of vibrant coordinating printed and plain cottons, but you could use any prints or colours you like. You could even turn this into an upcycling project. Choose bed linen, or any other textiles destined to be turned into something new.

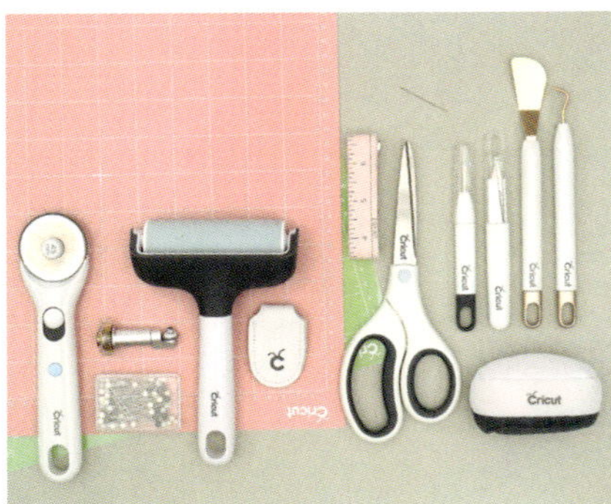

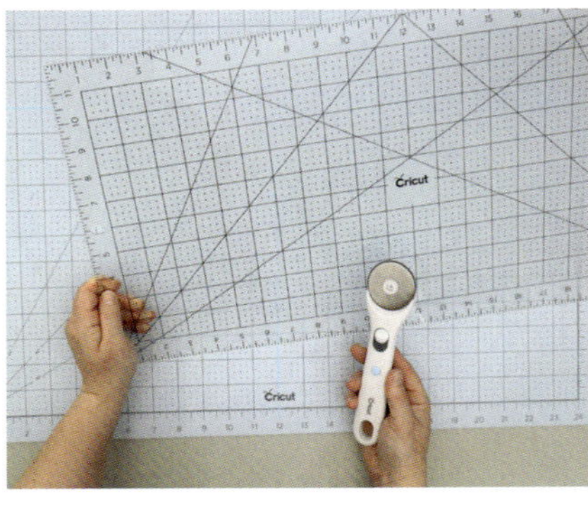

1 Using your scissors or hand-held rotary blade, trim your fabric to the right size for your FabricGrip Mat.

2 Use your brayer to attach the fabric on to your mat. Make sure there aren't any air bubbles or ridges in your fabric.

3 Add a hexagon to your Design Space Canvas and duplicate as necessary. The paper hexagons were cut at 2in (5cm) wide and the fabric hexagons 3in (7.5cm) wide. Load your fabric-loaded mat into your machine when requested and follow the on-screen instructions for cutting.

4 Once cut, unload your mat and weed away the bits between your hexagons. You can gently pull these away or use your weeder if necessary.

5 Pull your hexagons from the mat. You may find your spatula useful for this.

6 Repeat with the rest of your fabrics. I cut around 110 hexagons in total for a 16in (40.5cm) cushion.

7 Now select your StandardGrip Mat and add your paper. Use your brayer to ensure everything is nice and smooth and air-bubble free. You could use any medium weight cardstock – I simply like printed ones for fun while I'm sewing!

8 Follow the on-screen instructions for cutting.

9 Weed away the excess paper.

10 Remove the paper hexagons from your mat. You may find the spatula useful for this.

11 Bending the mat is also a handy tip.

12 Select some of your fabric hexagons and your paper hexagons. We will now 'baste' your hexagons. You could do this by sewing the fabric around each hexagon to tack into position, but I will be using the glue basting method.

13 Place one of your paper hexagons in the middle of the reverse side of one of your fabric hexagons.

14 Use your fabric glue along each edge of the paper hexagon.

15 Fold each fabric edge down over your hexagon to secure into position.

16 Continue working your way around the hexagon. Glue and fold into position...

17 ... until you have all edges folded into a hexagon.

18 Repeat with your other paper and fabric hexagons.

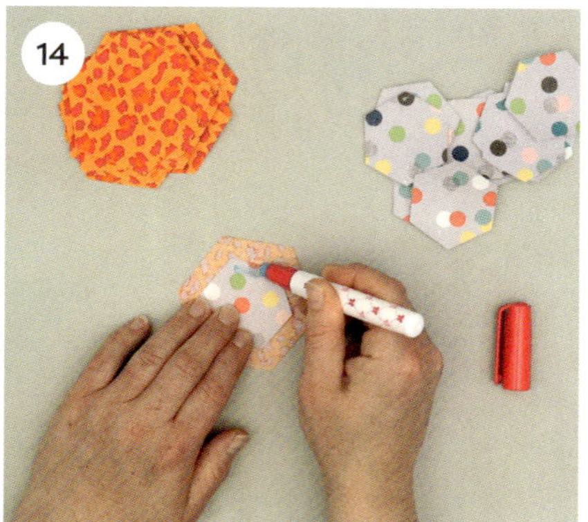

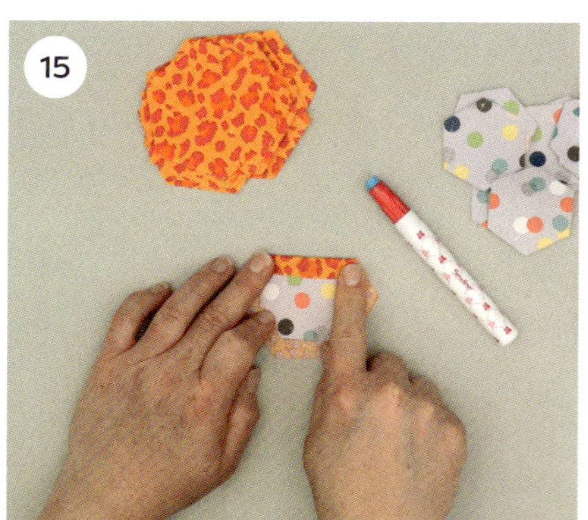

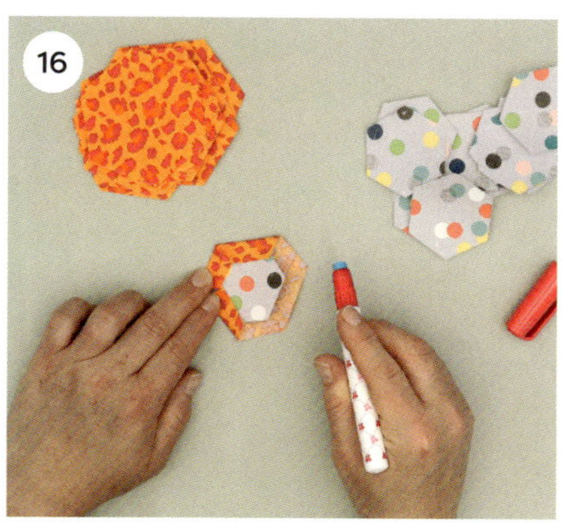

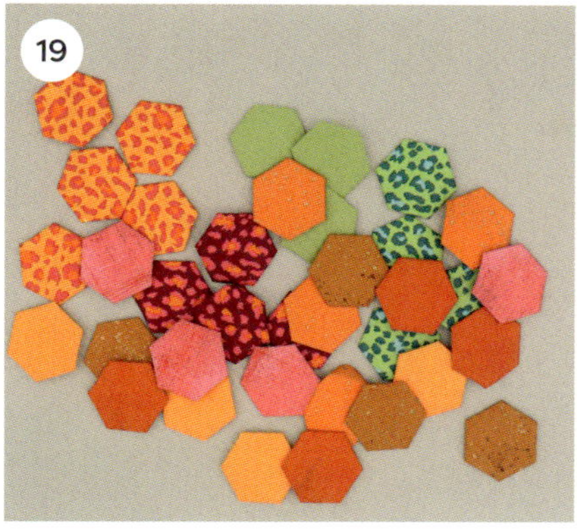

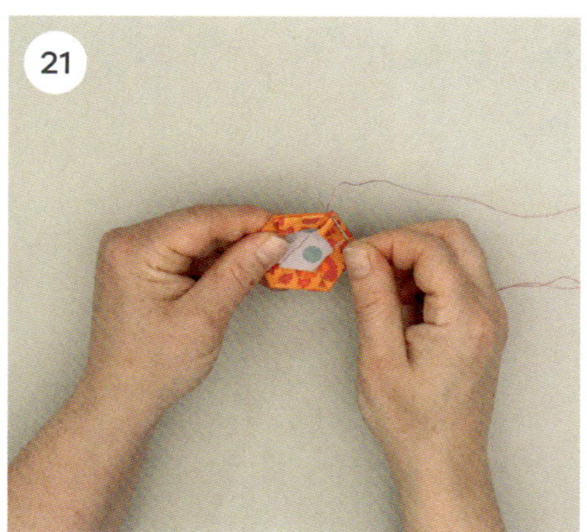

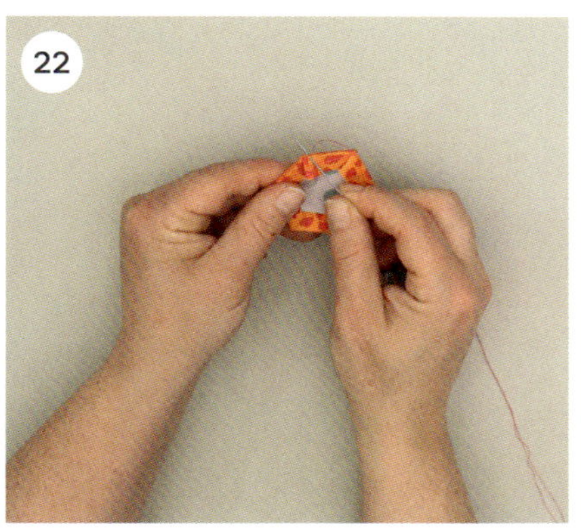

19 You are now ready to start hand sewing them all together.

20 Thread your needle and select two of your fabric-covered hexagons.

21 Place them right-side together, and push your needle through one corner of each hexagon together. You will need to stitch through the very edge of the fabric and not the paper. Go through over and back through each edge again. Push your needle up through the open loop to create a small knot. Do this knot at the start and end of each hexagon side.

22 Continue to go along the edge and make small stitches through both hexagons as above (but this time without the knot). Push your needle through the two layers of fabric along the hexagon edge joining them together, again, just at the very edge of the fabric and not through the paper. Pull your thread back over and then repeat by pushing your needle through again to start the next stitch slightly further along. Repeat this over and over working your way across. This is called 'whip stitch'.

23 Remember to make the small knot at the end of the hexagon edge, and now unfold outwards. You have two hexagons connected.

24 Repeat, attaching each hexagon in the same way.

25 Attach each side at a time, remembering to layer each one with right sides together.

26 You will need to fold some of the hexagons in half at times to be able to complete the whip stitch on some of the sides. Once you have attached three hexagons together you will start to see how it all comes together.

27 Repeat, continually adding hexagons, hand sewing each side together. To work with a continuous thread, make large tacking stitches on the back of the hexagons to get to the hexagon corner you need to start whip stitching again.

28 If you pick a central hexagon, you can work your way around to create a flower.

29 Snip your threads as you are going along.

30 Once you have an enclosed hexagon you can remove your paper template.

31 Keep sewing, adding hexagons as you go. I have chosen to mix and match prints and colour to create quite a bold and eclectic mix.

32 To create a 16in (40.5cm) cushion cover I kept measuring and checking with my tape measure to see whether I had enough sewn hexagons to meet the width and height. Adapt for whatever you are creating and make sure all of your paper templates are removed.

33 Once I was sure I had enough, I trimmed my sewing into a square. You could also add a one-sided fusible layer to the reverse side before trimming, to trap any loose threads.

34 Select your backing fabric. Cut two rectangles at two-thirds of the width of your cushion. I have cut two 16in (40.5cm) x 11in (28cm) rectangles. You now need to use your sewing machine to create seams on these rectangles.

35 Fold one of the 16in (40.5cm) edges over by around ⅜in (10mm) and again, so the raw edge is enclosed inside. Press if required.

36 Using a straight running stitch, sew into position.

31

32

33

34

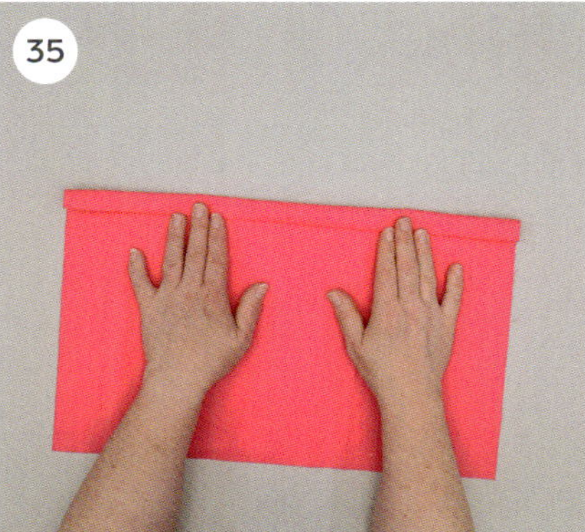
35

36

37 Place the rectangles down on to your hexagonal square, right sides together and overlapping the cushion backs. Pin into position if desired, before sewing around the edge. I used a straight running stitch and did two rounds of the cushion for extra stitch strength.

38 You will need to have a cushion inner. This one is 16in (40.5cm) square.

39 Turn your cushion cover out.

40 Push your corners out, and you are now ready for your cushion inner.

41 Push your cushion inner into position inside the cushion cover.

42 And you are done! One Cricut-cut, hand-sewn English Paper Pieced cushion.

GOING BEYOND THE MAKE

You could use this technique for any English Paper Piecing project – perhaps a bag, a bed runner, a quilt or even some clothing. It would make for a fabulous dressmaking project, such as a quilted jacket with larger hexagons. While it is easy to cut out hexagons in both paper and fabric by hand, using my Cricut machine ensures everything is precision-cut and cut out quickly, ready for me to start sewing and progressing with my project!

AFTERWORD

I hope that these 25 simple Cricut projects have allowed you to experiment with your new or existing Cricut machine(s)! And, that you have a new found confidence in the Cricut world. Things really are simple – when you know how.

If you make any of these projects, I would absolutely love to see!

Please do come and share your makes with me over on The Crafty Lass socials. It is certainly all about the Cricut community.

WEBSITE
www.thecraftylass.com

INSTAGRAM
@thecraftylass

FACEBOOK
The Crafty Lass

CRICUT DESIGN SPACE
https://design.cricut.com/landing/profile/5db42e1e4548dd05d0db3461

SUPPLIERS

Machines, Blades and Tools
Cricut.com

Paper and Card
Hobbycraft (hobbycraft.co.uk)
HobbyMaker (hobbymaker.com)
American Crafts (americancrafts.com)

Vinyl, Iron-On, Infusible Ink
Cricut.com
Hobbycraft (hobbycraft.co.uk)
Amazon (amazon.co.uk)

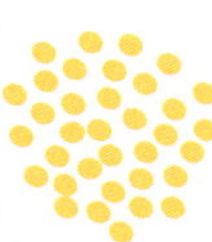

Blanks
Cricut.com
Dunelm (dunelm.com)
John Lewis & Waitrose (johnlewis.com)
Hobbycraft (hobbycraft.co.uk)
Habitat (habitat.co.uk)
Amazon (amazon.co.uk)
Cox & Cox (coxandcox.co.uk)
Longforte (longforte.com)

Sewing Machine
Brother Innovis NV1800Q

Fabrics
Craft Cotton Co at Hobbycraft (hobbycraft.co.uk)

Threads
Aurifil (aurifil.com)

ACKNOWLEDGEMENTS

Firstly, thank you to Kathy.

For that very first conversation and inviting me in to a whole new Cricut world. I didn't quite know what I was letting myself in for! And thank you for your genuine heartfelt excitement (and dancing!) when I told you about this book, and your absolute unequivocal support ever since.

Thank you to Kate (@themakerykate), for all of your support across the years. I still treasure my 'Make Amazing Things' tape measure. You are such a genuine and incredibly passionate person, and someone we all admire and certainly look up to.

Thank you to Fi (@katy_lou_designs), for everything you do for all of the Cricut ambassadors. #FiSentIt

Thank you to all of the Cricut team and my fellow Cricut UK ambassadors.

And a special thank you to Oriana – THIS is what the rose gold tools were for!

Thank you to Jonathan Bailey and the wider GMC team for asking me to write a second book, while also writing my first. Now that was a first – balancing writing two books almost at once.

And, as always, thank you to Dan... my lovely (not so Crafty) Lad, who is simply patient!

Thank you to my Mum and Dad who, just like me, can't believe I have a second book already.

And to my boys Freddie and Rupert, who really just want me to collect Cricut 'cuties' and make them a million things on 'Mummy's clever machines'.

While this book has not been produced in partnership with Cricut, the team has supported its creation, by offering guidance and advice, providing materials to test and ensuring the information is as up to date as possible.

First published 2025 by
Guild of Master Craftsman Publications Ltd
Castle Place, 166 High Street, Lewes,
East Sussex BN7 1XU

ISBN 978-1-78494-706-4

The publishers and author can accept no legal responsibility for any consequences arising from the application of information, advice or instructions given in this publication.

A catalogue record for this book is available from the British Library.

PUBLISHER Jonathan Bailey
PRODUCTION Jim Bulley
SENIOR PROJECT EDITOR Susie Behar
DESIGN MANAGER Robin Shields
EDITOR Alexis Harvey
DESIGN JC Lanaway

Photographs on pages 2, 3, 4, 32, 36, 42, 48, 53, 54, 58, 64, 70, 75, 76, 82, 87, 88, 93, 94, 98, 102, 108, 113, 114, 122, 129, 130, 136, 142, 147, 148, 153, 154, 158, 163, 164, 173 by **Andrew Perris**; Styling by **Anna Stevens**.
Author photograph Jenny Stewart Photography
All other photographs by the author.

Colour origination by GMC Reprographics
Printed and bound in China

GMC Publications Ltd
Castle Place, 166 High Street
Lewes, East Sussex
BN7 1XU
United Kingdom
Tel: +44 (0)1273 488005
www.gmcbooks.com